Past Masters
General Editor Keith Thomas

Adam Smith

D. D. Raphael is Emeritus Professor of Philosophy in
the University of London. His previous books include
Problems of Political Philosophy (1970) and *Moral
Philosophy* (OUP, 1981).

Past Masters

Forthcoming

and others

D. D. Raphael

Adam Smith

Oxford New York

OXFORD UNIVERSITY PRESS

Oxford University Press, Walton Street, Oxford OX2 6DP

Oxford New York Toronto
Delhi Bombay Calcutta Madras Karachi
Petaling Jaya Singapore Hong Kong Tokyo
Nairobi Dar es Salaam Cape Town
Melbourne Auckland

and associated companies in
Berlin Ibadan

Oxford is a trade mark of Oxford University Press

First published 1985 as an Oxford University Press paperback
and simultaneously in a hardback edition
Paperback reprinted 1987, 1989

British Library Cataloguing in Publication Data

Raphael, D. D.
Adam Smith.—(Past masters)
1. Smith, Adam, 1723–1790
2. Economics—Scotland—
History—18th century
I. Title II. Series
330.15'3 HB103.S6
ISBN 0–19–287558–2 Pbk

Library of Congress Cataloging in Publication Data

Raphael, D. D. (David Daiches), 1916–
Adam Smith.
(Past masters)
Bibliography: p. Includes index.
1. Smith Adam, 1723–1790. I. Title. II. Series.
HB103.S6R27 1985 330.15'3'0924 84–20629
ISBN 0–19–287558–2 (pbk.)

Printed in Great Britain by
The Guernsey Press Co. Ltd.
Guernsey, Channel Islands

Acknowledgements

I wish to thank the Leverhulme Trust for awarding me an Emeritus Fellowship to cover expenses incurred in writing this (and another) book.

I also wish to thank three people for their help. My wife, Sylvia Raphael, read the typescript and suggested a number of improvements in the presentation. My friend and former colleague at Glasgow University, Professor Andrew Skinner, to whose published work I was already indebted, kindly agreed to read Chapter 4 and gave me valuable advice on some particular points in my exposition of Adam Smith's economics. Ainslee Rutledge typed the text with great efficiency.

Some paragraphs of Chapter 6 repeat, in a revised form, part of a lecture on Adam Smith which I gave to the Royal Institute of Philosophy in a series called 'Philosophers of the Enlightenment' and subsequently published as a book with that title.

D.D.R.

Contents

Abbreviations

All page references in the text are to The Glasgow Edition of the Works and Correspondence of Adam Smith, published by the Clarendon Press, Oxford. Abbreviations are as follows:

M   *The Theory of Moral Sentiments*, ed. D. D. Raphael and A. L. Macfie (1976)

W   *An Inquiry into the Nature and Causes of the Wealth of Nations*, general editors R. H. Campbell and A. S. Skinner, textual editor W. B. Todd (1976)

P   *Essays on Philosophical Subjects*, ed. W. P. D. Wightman, J. C. Bryce, and I. S. Ross, general editors D. D. Raphael and A. S. Skinner (1980)

R   *Lectures on Rhetoric and Belles Lettres*, ed. J. C. Bryce, general editor A. S. Skinner (1983)

J   *Lectures on Jurisprudence*, ed. R. L. Meek, D. D. Raphael, and P. G. Stein (1978)

C   *The Correspondence of Adam Smith*, ed. E. C. Mossner and I. S. Ross (1977)

1 A master for many schools

Adam Smith is a past master for all manner of persons, for Conservatives and for Marxists, for liberals and for anti-radicals, for economists, philosophers, and sociologists. Different groups admire different things in his work and one may sometimes doubt whether all the different things can be held together consistently. Still, each of them is persuasive enough to have made its mark as a truth of some profundity.

An Inquiry into the Nature and Causes of the Wealth of Nations is best known for its advocacy of free trade. Nineteenth-century liberals believed, like Adam Smith himself, that freedom of trade goes hand in hand with other kinds of freedom and adopted it as a cardinal principle of policy. More recently their clothes have been stolen by the Conservatives, and in Britain at least, since the end of the Second World War, the most fervent disciples of a free-market economy have been leading lights of the Conservative party. When in May 1979 Sir Keith Joseph took office as Secretary of State for Industry in Mrs Thatcher's first government, he sent round to his senior civil servants a 'reading list' which included both the *Wealth of Nations* and Adam Smith's earlier book, *The Theory of Moral Sentiments*.

It is not surprising that right-wing politicians should praise a work which finds in capitalism the root of all economic good. It is surprising, at first sight, that Karl Marx should be indebted to the *Wealth of Nations*; but the reasons are clear enough. Marx's materialist interpretation of history is a theory of stages of society, each having a distinctive social structure in terms of property and depending on a distinctive system of production. The essence of such a theory underlies the *Wealth of Nations*, which is as much a sociological as an economic treatise. Smith writes of four stages of society, beginning with an age of hunters, followed by one of shepherds, and then proceeding through an age of agriculture to an age of commerce. The analysis of economic activity, which forms the main subject of the book, belongs to the fourth stage of the process. The historical picture is intended to explain the development of law and government, which, according to this account, are first needed in the age of shepherds, when the concept of property arises. Hunters consume at once what they catch; shepherds tend flocks for future as well as present use. Property has to be protected, and this, in Smith's view, is the primary aim of government. 'Civil government, so far as it is instituted for the security of property, is in reality instituted for the defence of the rich against the poor, or of those who have some property against those who have none at all' (W 715). Adam Smith is not the only writer in whom Marx will have read of stages in the history of human society, but none struck a more radical note than this.

Yet Adam Smith can also be quoted by opponents of radicalism, at any rate of political radicalism. 'The man of system', Smith wrote, 'is apt to be very wise in his own conceit; and is often so enamoured with the supposed beauty of his own ideal plan of government, that he cannot suffer the smallest deviation from any part of it' (M 233-4). He thinks he can arrange society like the pieces on a chess-board and forgets that 'in the great chess-board of human society, every single piece has a principle of motion of its own, altogether different from that which the legislature might chuse to impress upon it.' We are back to arguments for freedom, this time political freedom, but a conception of political freedom that goes against the reforming radicalism of constitution makers.

James Boswell was once a student of Adam Smith at the University of Glasgow. In later years Smith told Boswell that his great fault was acting upon system and Boswell thought this was strange criticism to come from a philosopher. As a philosopher, and indeed as an economist, Smith certainly sought system but he kept it in its proper place. Systematic theory was one thing, essential for satisfactory explanation. Acting upon system, a necessarily simplified system, without regarding the practicalities of the individual case, was quite another thing.

Adam Smith did not found the study, even the scientific study, of economics. Ancient and medieval thinkers had glimpses of some economic truths in their reflections on the workings of human society. In the seventeenth century, and in the eighteenth before the publication of the *Wealth of Nations*, there were significant advances in constructing theories of value, of money, and of international trade. Mercantilism, the doctrine which advocated governmental control of foreign trade, developed a systematic theory, notably in the treatises of Thomas Mun in the seventeenth century and of Smith's fellow-Scotsman Sir James Steuart a few years (1767) before the publication of the *Wealth of Nations* (1776). In France the physiocrats had worked out a very different account of economic activity, favouring a policy of free trade. While the origins of their doctrine depended on philosophical ideas of natural law, it was turned into a scientific system by François Quesnay with his *Tableau économique* (1758). This was a quasi-physiological model of the annual flow of payments from one class of citizens to another, in the form of rent, prices, wages, profits. It was probably conceived on the analogy of

3

the circulation of the blood (Quesnay was trained and practised as a doctor) and was a landmark in the history of economics as a systematic enquiry. Quesnay had been influenced by an earlier work (1755) of Richard Cantillon, which some scholars regard as the first scientific treatment of the principles of economics.

The *Wealth of Nations* is much more comprehensive in scope and more detailed in its factual data than these French models. Despite that, it is remarkably systematic in connecting together different features of what we would now call the economic life of society. The book is impressive, as Darwin's *On the Origin of Species* is impressive, for combining a systematic theory with a wealth of illustrative empirical data. But the systematic character of the theory is a matter of showing connections rather than focusing upon a single explanatory principle, as Darwin does. Smith's appeal to the 'obvious and simple system of natural liberty' (W 687), criticizing mercantilism, expresses a deep-seated ideological conviction, but he does not use it as a universal principle to explain all economic activity. The *Wealth of Nations* put all earlier treatises of political economy in the shade because it was so comprehensively systematic, not because it blew the trumpet of free trade. It became the standard model to be studied, tested, revised, and improved.

More recent economists have looked at the work from a different angle. Their attention to economic growth has led them to see that Smith's *Inquiry into the Nature and Causes of the Wealth of Nations* is, as the full title implies, an examination of economic growth or development and so continues to be in the mainstream of economic thought as envisaged today. The book begins with the division of labour in order to bring out sharply from the start the enormous difference in productivity between the manufacture of a pin by one man and the sharing of the process by ten men. Smith then goes on to relate the division of labour to the accumulation of capital, the increase of employment, and a self-regulating mechanism for preventing wages from rising too high to inhibit further growth. In this perspective of economic growth, Smith's sociological excursus on the history of society, with its four stages of development, falls into place as the essential background of his picture.

The sociological interest of Smith's work is not, however, confined to his theory of social history. In the *Wealth of Nations* there are striking disquisitions on education, on the clergy, on the character of different classes in society, on the psychological effects of specialization. If the reader of the *Wealth of Nations* also reads *The Theory of Moral Sentiments*, he will see that the whole of Smith's thought on human behaviour is permeated by a sociological approach. The *Moral Sentiments*, primarily a book of moral philosophy, deals with morality as a social phenomenon. In Smith's account of ethics the central place is given to sympathy, the cement of society. The resulting approval or disapproval of other people for what a man does is the mirror in which he sees his own character. While Smith's economics follow up the social effects of self-interested behaviour conditioned by the market, his ethics point to the equally firm structure of social solidarity built up by sympathy and our desire for esteem.

The *Moral Sentiments* remains a work of philosophy for all that. It stands out as a peak in the history of one type of ethical theory, basing moral values on human feelings. Adam Smith's book is less widely read nowadays than the slightly earlier work of his friend David Hume. If one thinks of their respective contributions to philosophy generally, Smith comes nowhere near the eminence of Hume (of which Smith himself had a warm appreciation). If, however, one thinks of moral philosophy in particular, the honours are shared more evenly. Smith followed up and improved upon Hume's highlighting of the role of sympathy in ethics; and then he added his own, more distinctive, concept of an imagined 'impartial spectator' to explain conscience, the moral judgements that a person makes about his own actions. The theory resembles that which Freud was to produce, in the twentieth century, of the super-ego, but with the difference that Smith begins with social approval and disapproval while Freud begins with parental.

Among scholars of the history and philosophy of science, those who also go into the history of their own subject know that Adam Smith is one of the pioneers in that field with his essay 'The History of Astronomy'. It is philosophical as well as historical. In both respects the essay is outstanding for its time. The historical treatment is now outdated but the accompanying philosophical theory, which takes scientific systems to be products of the imagination, still arouses admiration as a remarkably bold feat of Smith's own rational imagination.

Both in his ethical theory and in his philosophy of science Smith's strength lies in philosophical psychology. This will be apparent from his emphasis on sympathy and imagination and from my comparison with Freud. The theories of philosophical psychology, whether they come from professed philosophers or from would-be scientists like Freud, contain a speculative element and are not easily confirmed or refuted by hard empirical data. Adam Smith, however, impresses his readers as an empirical psychologist too. Both in the *Moral Sentiments* and in the *Wealth of Nations* he shows himself an acute observer of behaviour.

The mob, when they are gazing at a dancer on the slack rope, naturally writhe and twist and balance their own bodies, as they see him do, and as they feel that they themselves must do if in his situation. (M 10)

A bully tells many stories of his own insolence, which are not true, and imagines that he thereby renders himself, if not more amiable and respectable, at least more formidable to his audience. (M 240)

Two greyhounds, in running down the same hare, have sometimes the appearance of acting in some sort of concert. Each turns her towards his companion, or endeavours to intercept her when his companion turns her towards himself. (W 25)

The social anthropologist Edward Westermarck described the *Moral Sentiments* as 'the most important contribution to moral psychology made by any British thinker'. The historian H. T. Buckle said of the *Wealth of Nations*: 'looking at its ultimate results, [it] is probably the most important book that has ever been written, and is certainly the most valuable contribution ever made by a single man towards establishing the principles on which government should be based.' The first opinion is no more than just; the second is rather wild, though by no means ridiculous. The two together illustrate the enthusiasm that Adam Smith has kindled in different quarters as a past master.

2 Life

Adam Smith was born in Kirkcaldy on the Fife coast. The precise date of his birth is uncertain but he was baptized on 5 June 1723. He was a posthumous child, his father having died in January of that year. The father, also named Adam, was a lawyer and civil servant. He was twice married and had one son from each marriage. His first wife, Lilias Drummond, died in 1717, when her son Hugh was about eight years old. His second wife, mother of the famous Adam, was Margaret Douglas. Their marriage took place in 1720, when she was in her twenties and he was about forty. She was widowed after less than three years. In such circumstances an only child, born after the death of her husband, must have been doubly precious, and the ties between mother and son remained exceptionally close for the rest of her long life. Adam Smith himself never married and Freudians will no doubt say that this was the consequence of the bond with his mother. However, filial affection did not stop him from falling in love at least twice and his susceptibility is plain enough in passages of the *Moral Sentiments*.

There is a tale that at the age of three Adam Smith was stolen by a band of gypsies when he was visiting his uncle. His biographer, John Rae, writes 'He would have made, I fear, a poor gipsy', no doubt thinking of Smith's notorious absent-mindedness as well as his bent for speculative thought. I am not sure that Adam Smith himself would have agreed. He thought that abilities owed more to nurture than to nature. 'The difference between the most dissimilar characters, between a philosopher and a common street porter, for example, seems to arise not so much from nature, as from habit, custom, and education' (W 28-9). In any event, Smith is not the only absent-minded professor to be eminently successful at practical administration and I dare say he could have been a very useful member of a gypsy band. However, his enforced sojourn with them lasted only a few hours.

After attending the burgh school in Kirkcaldy, Smith entered the University of Glasgow in 1737 at the age of fourteen, a little older than was usual in those days to begin university studies. Why he was sent to Glasgow rather than to one of the nearer universities at Edinburgh or St Andrews is not known. It may have been because he had an aunt living in Glasgow or it may have been because the University of Glasgow offered the opportunity of going on to Balliol College, Oxford, with the Snell Exhibition, as Smith in fact did. One of his fellow-students recalled in later years that Smith's favourite subjects at Glasgow University were mathematics and natural philosophy (physics). His competence in those subjects is shown in his essay on the history of astronomy but his works generally do not suggest a particular bent in that direction. The strongest influence on Smith as a student was that of Francis Hutcheson, the Professor of Moral Philosophy, whose lectures on ethics, jurisprudence, and economics laid the foundations of Smith's own ideas in those areas.

From Glasgow Smith proceeded to Oxford in 1740 with a Snell Exhibition, an award originally intended to support the training of Scottish students for the ministry of 'the Church in Scotland', meaning the Episcopal Church. That requirement of the benefaction was nullified when the Church of Scotland became Presbyterian in 1690, and in Adam Smith's time, as today, the Snell Exhibition was available for talented students of Glasgow University to go to Oxford and study whatever they wished. Smith was at Oxford for six years and his studies seem to have been largely self-directed. Like Edward Gibbon, he found the teachers at Oxford University scandalously idle and incompetent. He wrote in the *Wealth of Nations* (761): 'In the university of Oxford, the greater part of the publick professors have, for these many years, given up altogether even the pretence of teaching.' There could hardly be a greater contrast with Glasgow, where teaching had the first priority and where Hutcheson in particular was a brilliant lecturer.

However, at Balliol College Smith had the run of a good library and he read widely in Greek and Latin classics and in French literature (passages from which he enjoyed translating into English). He also read a certain amount of modern philosophy, including the recently published *Treatise of Human Nature* by his fellow-Scotsman, Hume. Smith told his friends in later years that he was reprimanded when found reading this book at Oxford and that the work itself was confiscated. The *Treatise* was generally regarded as atheistic and subversive of morality. Smith himself seems to have had a shrewder understanding of some of its more original features. His references to Hume's ethics in *The Theory of Moral Sentiments* show a perceptive, if not altogether accurate, recollection of parts of the *Treatise*, and his essay on the history of astronomy depends on a grasp of Hume's subtle theory of the imagination which eluded most professional philosophers for a couple of centuries.

From Oxford Smith returned to his mother's house in Kirkcaldy and no doubt explored the possibilities of earning his living. Two years later, arrangements were made by a group of well-wishers in Edinburgh, including a leading member of the Scottish Bar, Henry Home (later a judge with the title Lord Kames), for Smith to give a series of public lectures on rhetoric and *belles-lettres*. The lectures were not part of any university course in Edinburgh, but were well attended, mostly by students of law and theology, and were continued in the following two years, bringing Smith an annual income of over £100. In at least the last of the three years, Smith added to the lectures on rhetoric and *belles-lettres* a further series on civil law for the benefit of his law students. The lectures were attended also by a number of older people prominent in the cultural life of the city.

They made a great impression and when the Chair of Logic at the University of Glasgow became vacant at the end of 1750, Smith was at once offered the appointment and took it up in 1751, supplementing the customary account of logic and metaphysics with a treatment of rhetoric and *belles-lettres* such as he had given in Edinburgh. He thought this subject would be 'more interesting and useful' to his students (P 273). There was, however, another good reason for making use of his Edinburgh lectures. In the summer of 1751, before Smith began his teaching duties, the Professor of Moral Philosophy was taken ill and was advised to go abroad to a warmer climate for the winter. Smith was asked to take over part of the Moral Philosophy course in addition to his work with the Logic class. The people at Glasgow knew that Smith's successful lectures in Edinburgh had included a discussion of law and government, and so it was suggested that his contribution to the lectures of the Moral Philosophy class should be the parts on 'natural jurisprudence and politics' (C 5). Since he had to take on this additional commitment in his first year of teaching, it was obviously convenient to ease the burden by using the material of his Edinburgh lectures for part of his Logic course too.

Smith's tenure in the Chair of Logic was short-lived. The ailing Professor of Moral Philosophy, Thomas Craigie, died in November 1751 and in the following April Smith was appointed to succeed him. The subjects covered in the Moral Philosophy class (theology, ethics, general principles of law and government, economics) were more to his taste than logic and metaphysics, although he continued, in his new post, to give his course on rhetoric and literature as an addition to the regular course of moral philosophy. A student report of the rhetoric lectures in the 1762-3 session came to light in 1958, together with a similar report of the second half of the moral philosophy course. A summarized report of the lectures on 'jurisprudence' (law, government, and economics), as delivered in 1763-4, had previously been made known in 1895.

Adam Smith held the Chair of Moral Philosophy at Glasgow for twelve years. He was an admirable professor. Although he could not match the eloquence of Hutcheson, his own teacher and Craigie's predecessor, Smith had a gift for clear exposition and happy illustration, and his actual theories showed more originality, greater coherence, and a sharper awareness of difficulties than did the theories of Hutcheson. Like Hutcheson, Smith took his responsibilities to his students very seriously indeed. He gave his regular or 'public' course of lectures at an early hour on each weekday, followed it up with an informal discussion or 'examination' later in the morning, and then delivered his additional or 'private' course on rhetoric at midday. He gave individual tutorials to selected pupils and showed meticulous concern for the health and personal development of students who were private boarders in his house. Smith was outstanding also in university administration. He undertook far more of such work than the average professor and was judged to be especially capable at it. He was College Quaestor (Treasurer) for six years, a much longer period than usual, and towards the end of his time at Glasgow he acted as Dean of Faculty, Vice-Rector, and chairman of a special committee set up to try to resolve a long-standing wrangle about the respective powers of the Principal and the Rector. Whenever the university had to undertake ticklish negotiations with outside bodies such as the town council in Glasgow or the Treasury in London, more often than not it asked Smith to act as its spokesman. Despite his reputation for absent-mindedness, he was clearly hard-headed and efficient in matters of practical business.

Smith's lectures on moral philosophy were divided into three sections, natural theology, ethics, and jurisprudence. This followed the practice of his predecessors and indeed the general tradition of Scottish moral philosophy of the period.

Of the content of his lectures on natural theology we know virtually nothing. A report by John Millar, originally a pupil and then a colleague and friend, says simply that in this part of his course Smith 'considered the proofs of the being and attributes of God, and those principles of the human mind upon which religion is founded' (P 274). Some inkling of his approach to the latter topic is given in one chapter of the *Moral Sentiments*, where he talks of divinities as originally the object of religious fear and as conceived to resemble human beings in their sentiments and passions. The suggestion here that man creates gods in his own image may explain a complaint that was made by some people to the effect that Smith's lectures on natural theology 'were too flattering to human pride'.

The second part of his lectures, on ethics, was eventually turned into *The Theory of Moral Sentiments*. Smith's inclination in the study of any subject was to approach it historically in the first instance and then to form his own ideas from reflections on past history. There is reason to think that his lectures on ethics in their earliest form began with a historical survey of moral philosophy from Plato to Hume. In his own ethical theory he starts from the same base as Hutcheson, his teacher, and Hume, by now his friend, but moving in a new direction to accommodate weaknesses in their positions. There is also clear evidence that Smith's ethical theory developed significantly in the course of his twelve years as Professor of Moral Philosophy, both before and after the publication of the first edition of *The Theory of Moral Sentiments* in 1759.

The third part of his lectures, on jurisprudence, is described by John Millar as a third and fourth part, the third dealing with 'justice' in the form of a history of law and government, and the fourth dealing with 'expediency', the subject-matter of the *Wealth of Nations*. It seems, however, that at first Smith did not think of economics as something separate from the history of law and society. He included both in his lectures on 'jurisprudence', as can be seen from the two reports that we have of those lectures, a full but incomplete recital of the lectures of 1762-3, and a more summary but complete account of the lectures of 1763-4. Economics is a central feature of the workings of society and Smith believed that evidence of its development could often best be found in the history of changes in the law. The basic attitude, historical and sociological with liberty as the leading value, owed much to Montesquieu, and the detailed account of legal and economic structure was built upon a foundation inherited again from Hutcheson; but Smith's own advance upon them, in working out a firm, complex, and coherent theory of social change and economic process, is far more marked than his originality in ethical theory and is plain for all to see. As with his lectures on ethics, there is evidence that Smith was actively developing both his economic theory and his history of law in the annual delivery of his lectures.

One of Smith's own remarks about his lecturing procedure has been recorded. In order to gauge the interest of his audience, he used to keep his eye on one student whom he judged to have a specially expressive face. 'If he leant forward to listen all was right, and I knew that I had the ear of my class; but if he leant back in an attitude of listlessness I felt at once that all was wrong, and that I must change either the subject or the style of my address.'

There is some conflict of evidence about another of Smith's habits concerning his lectures. When he died in 1790, an anonymous obituary notice in the *Gentleman's Magazine* mentioned that during his professorship at Glasgow he was afraid of plagiarism and would say, when he saw students taking notes, 'I hate scribblers.' On the other hand John Millar, who was undoubtedly in a position to know, wrote of 'the permission given to students of taking notes', in consequence of which many of Smith's observations in his rhetoric lectures had become known through the works of others (P 274). The reports which we now have of very full notes taken by a student (or two students) of Smith's courses of lectures in the 1762-3 session make it difficult to believe the story in the obituary notice. A different interpretation of that tale appears in an anonymous biography of Smith, prefixed to a Glasgow edition of the *Moral Sentiments* in 1809 and probably written by one of Smith's former colleagues. The author says that Smith was 'uneasy when he observed notes of [his lectures] taken down in his class' because 'to be sufficiently full, they must be written with a haste which precludes any thing like accuracy, and, if shewn about in this state, the errors are as likely to be imputed to the original as to the copy'.

The students themselves had no complaints to make about Smith's practices in his lectures. Quite the contrary. When he left the university in 1764, it was in the middle of the academic session, and although he arranged for a substitute to read the rest of his lectures on his behalf, he nevertheless thought it proper to return to his students the fees they had paid for the year. (Fees were paid directly to the professor of each class and formed the major part of his salary.) The students protested vigorously. The first one called up to be given back his money 'peremptorily refused to accept it, declaring that the instruction and pleasure he had already received was much more than he either had repaid or ever could compensate, and a general cry was heard from every one in the room to the same effect'. Smith, however, insisted that his conscience demanded that the fees be returned and thrust the money into the young man's pocket.

By this time Smith had acquired a considerable reputation, both in Britain and on the continent of Europe, through the publication in 1759 of *The Theory of Moral Sentiments*. The immediate success of the book in London is described by David Hume in one of the most delightful of his letters. After tantalizing Smith with tales of interruptions, he prefaces his account of the book's reception with the warning that philosophy can be properly appreciated only by a select few and that 'the approbation of the multitude' is more likely to attend falsehood than truth.

Supposing, therefore, that you have duely prepard yourself for the worst by all these Reflections; I proceed to tell you the melancholy News, that your Book has been very unfortunate: For the Public seem disposd to applaud it extremely. It was lookd for by the foolish People with some Impatience; and the Mob of Literati are beginning already to be very loud in its Praises. Three Bishops calld yesterday at Millar's Shop in order to buy Copies, and to ask Questions about the Author: The Bishop of Peterborough said he had passd the Evening in a Company, where he heard it extolld above all Books in the World. You may conclude what Opinion true Philosophers will entertain of it, when these Retainers to Superstition praise it so highly. . . . Millar exults and brags that two thirds of the Edition are already sold, and that he is now sure of Success. You see what a Son of the Earth that is, to value Books only by the Profit they bring him. In that View, I believe it may prove a very good Book. (C 35)

Despite the implied hint, made not altogether with tongue in cheek, that from a strictly philosophical point of view Hume might not regard it as 'a very good book', he was genuinely pleased that his friend should enjoy a literary success which his own first book had never had. He went on to say that one of the leading lights impressed by the work was Charles Townshend, who talked of placing his stepson, the young Duke of Buccleuch, under the tutelage of Adam Smith when going abroad on the customary grand tour for his education. Four years later Townshend made Smith a formal offer to that effect and as a result Smith gave up his Glasgow Chair. The terms of Townshend's proposal were a salary of £500 per annum, to be followed, after the grand tour was over, by a pension for life of £300 per annum (probably more than Smith earned at Glasgow).

The fame of the *Moral Sentiments* quickly spread beyond Britain. It was read and admired in the literary circles of Paris and was quite soon translated into French. It was sufficiently known in Geneva for Dr Théodore Tronchin, a distinguished physician in that city, to decide in 1761 to send his son to Glasgow University to be taught by Adam Smith. In the same year two students, S. E. Desnitsky and I. A. Tret'yakov, came from Moscow for the same purpose. Both of them must have taken back a full report of Smith's lectures on jurisprudence, since their own lectures as professors of law in the University of Moscow include a repetition of Smith's views very close to the wording of the manuscript reports of Smith's jurisprudence lectures in 1762-3 and in 1763-4.

Smith's residence in Glasgow gave him ample opportunity to meet the merchants of the town, engaged especially in the thriving tobacco trade. He was a regular attender at three clubs, the most important of which was the Political Economy Club, founded by Andrew Cochrane, a leading merchant and banker, 'to inquire into the nature and principles of trade in all its branches'. In later years, when Smith was collecting detailed information for the *Wealth of Nations*, he acknowledged a debt to Cochrane for some of it. Discussions with Cochrane and other prominent Glasgow merchants such as William Cunninghame, Alexander Spiers, John Glassford, and James Ritchie must have given Smith a feel for the real world of commerce. It is worth noting, however, that his belief in the virtues of free trade owed nothing to them. Their own experience led them to support mercantilism. The striking growth of trade at Glasgow in the middle of the eighteenth century was greatly assisted by the protection of the Navigation Acts. Yet it seems, according to the testimony of one of these merchants, James Ritchie, that Smith converted many of them to the doctrine of free trade.

Adam Smith left Glasgow in January 1764 to take up his new post of tutor to the Duke of Buccleuch. The two left for

France in February and after spending a few days in Paris proceeded to Toulouse, where they remained for eighteen months. Introductions to local people went slowly at first and life was dull, so much so, said Smith in a letter, that 'I have begun to write a book in order to pass away the time' (C 102). This does not mean that the project of writing the *Wealth of Nations* originated in Toulouse. At the end of the *Moral Sentiments* Smith had announced an intention of producing 'another discourse' on 'the general principles of law and government' (M 342), which would doubtless have included economics as a part of government, following the pattern of his lectures on jurisprudence. Some time later he must have decided to write about economics separately, since there is a manuscript draft of an early version of the first part of the *Wealth of Nations*, written before Smith's last session at Glasgow. A letter from the Glasgow merchant John Glassford, sent to Smith in France towards the end of 1764, expresses the hope that he is getting on with 'the usefull work that was so well advanced here' (C 104).

After a few months Smith began to find his feet in getting to know people in France and in speaking the language. The Duke of Buccleuch's younger brother, Hew Scott, joined them in the autumn. They visited several places in the South of France and then, in October 1765, they moved to Geneva, where they stayed for two months. At Geneva Dr Tronchin would have introduced Smith to everyone who counted, including Voltaire, whom Smith met on five or six occasions. Smith had an enormous respect for Voltaire, not only as the scourge of fanatics but also as a writer. His admiration of Voltaire's tragedies is excessive but he had good reason to appreciate Voltaire's services as a publicist in the cause of justice. In the last edition of the *Moral Sentiments* Smith writes movingly of the trial of the

Protestant, Jean Calas, who was mistakenly convicted and executed at Toulouse in 1762 on a charge of having murdered his son. The protest of Voltaire was mainly responsible for the eventual decision to conduct a judicial re-examination of the case in March 1765, when the earlier verdict was overturned. The result was not well received by the local townspeople, and Smith must have heard much acrimonious discussion of the matter during his stay in Toulouse.

From Geneva Smith and his young charges went to Paris, where they arrived at the beginning of 1766 and remained until the end of October. In Paris their social life was as hectic as it had been dull in Toulouse. High society among the British community in Paris was of course completely open to a Duke and stepson of the politician Charles Townshend. Smith himself had his own lines of entry to British and French notables through his friendship with Hume, who had just left Paris after having been in charge of the British embassy. Like Hume, Smith was popular with the literary ladies of the Paris salons. One of them, Madame Riccoboni, an actress and successful novelist, wrote of him in letters to David Garrick: 'j'aime Mr Smith, je l'aime beaucoup. Je voudrais que le diable emportât tous nos gens de lettres, tous nos philosophes, et qu'il me rapportât Mr Smith.' 'Vous verrez un philosophe moral et pratique; gay, riant, à cent lieues de la pédanterie des nôtres.' And again, referring to Smith's forgetfulness: 'c'est la plus distraite créature! mais c'est une des plus aimables.'

In addition to the salons Smith enjoyed regular attendance at the theatre in Paris. But he found time for more serious pursuits too. He was frequently at gatherings of the group of French economists known as physiocrats. Their leader Quesnay was physician to the King and they used to meet at Quesnay's apartments in Paris or Versailles.

The physiocrats held that agriculture was the only source of national wealth because it alone yielded a genuine surplus over the costs of production; other forms of production made use of the products of agriculture and turned them into consumable goods. Government policy should therefore give priority to agriculture instead of to manufacture and trade, as the mercantilists believed. One of the younger members of the group, Dupont de Nemours, later edited the works of Turgot and in one of his notes he referred to Adam Smith as having been a 'fellow-disciple' of Quesnay in Paris. Smith was not a disciple of Quesnay. The principles of his thought on economics had been worked out long before he came to France. These principles included freedom of trade and the view that the real wealth of a country does not consist in money but in commodities, doctrines which he shared with the physiocrats in opposition to mercantilism, but if he owed them to anyone it was to Hutcheson and Hume, not Quesnay. He was of course prepared to learn from the French economists, as they were from him. He did not agree with their basic tenet about the overriding importance of agriculture but he thought well enough of them to say in the *Wealth of Nations* (678) that their system 'is, perhaps, the nearest approximation to the truth that has yet been published upon the subject of political oeconomy'. He had a great personal respect for Quesnay and originally intended to dedicate the *Wealth of Nations* to him, but by the time it appeared Quesnay was dead.

The warmth of Smith's feeling for Quesnay depended on more than their mutual interest in economics. When the Duke of Buccleuch and later his brother Hew fell ill, Quesnay agreed to Smith's requests that he should attend them personally. The Duke recovered from his fever in the summer but Hew Scott's illness in October proved fatal.

Smith himself scarcely ever left the young man's bedside. In addition to Quesnay and the doctor at the British embassy, Smith summoned the aid of his old friend Tronchin of Geneva, but their efforts were vain. Smith's letters to Lady Frances Scott, sister of his two pupils, are deeply moving expressions of his concern and care, as is the mere fact that he wrote to her rather than her stepfather, so that she might break the news to her mother in the way she thought best. The death of Hew put an end to the sojourn in France. Smith and the Duke of Buccleuch returned to London with Hew's body on 1 November 1766.

A few months later Smith went back to his mother's house in Kirkcaldy. He remained there until 1773, working with little interruption on his book. He had hoped to complete it well before that time. A letter from Hume in February 1770 implies that Smith is about to set off for London to look after the publication. In fact Smith did not go to London until April 1773, and even then revision occupied him for almost three more years. However, these London years were not so entirely taken up with working on the book. He consorted with fellow Scots at the British Coffee House and with a distinguished circle of English worthies at the Literary Club: Sir Joshua Reynolds, Edward Gibbon, Edmund Burke, Samuel Johnson and his shadow James Boswell, Oliver Goldsmith, Sir William Jones the orientalist, and David Garrick. It seems that his companions at the Club found his conversation instructive rather than lively, a very different picture from that conveyed by the literary ladies of Paris. Perhaps he had become a dull dog in the intervening years, weighed down by the mass of material facts with which he was dealing in his book; or perhaps the picture is distorted because most of the evidence comes from Boswell, who by this time had lost his affection for his old professor, now 'a professed infidel' and a man whose relations with Johnson were marked with coolness on both sides. A more agreeable vignette of Adam Smith in London was given by Benjamin Franklin, who said that Smith read each chapter of the *Wealth of Nations* to him, Richard Price (moral philosopher and writer on public finance), and others, listening patiently to their criticisms and then bringing back to them revised versions of what he had written. Smith will certainly have obtained much valuable information about America from Franklin, just as he had obtained information about France from his observations in that country and from his friendship with Quesnay, Turgot, and other physiocrats. However, in a letter he once dismissed Richard Price, quite unfairly, as 'a factious citizen, a most superficial Philosopher and by no means an able calculator' (C 290).

The *Wealth of Nations* eventually appeared on 9 March 1776. It met with immediate and resounding success. Smith's friends were all loud in their praises of its merits but thought that such a learned and complex work could not possibly be popular. They were wrong. The original edition was sold out in six months. The first volume of Gibbon's *Decline and Fall of the Roman Empire* had been produced by the same publisher a few weeks earlier. Hume said, both to Smith and to the publisher Strahan, that while both books were excellent, Smith's required 'too much thought' to be as popular as Gibbon's; but Gibbon himself hit upon the reason why the sale of the *Wealth of Nations* exceeded expectations: 'the most profound ideas expressed in the most perspicuous language'. The book sets out a highly complicated skein of thought but almost always expressed in remarkably simple terms, with homely illustrations and a great number of memorably vivid maxims. Would that economists today could recover the art!

Hume's initial reaction to the *Wealth of Nations*, though less amusing than his letter about the *Moral Sentiments*, deserves quotation for the warmth and sincerity of its first words. While Hume did not write a book on economics, his own contributions to the subject showed the same penetrating intelligence that is familiar to students of his philosophical work. The first two words of his letter express unparalleled enthusiasm. The first is Greek, the second Latin, meaning 'Well done! Splendid!'

> Euge! Belle! Dear Mr Smith: I am much pleas'd with your Performance, and the Perusal of it has taken me from a State of great Anxiety. It was a Work of so much Expectation, by yourself, by your Friends, and by the Public, that I trembled for its Appearance; but am now much relieved. Not but that the Reading of it necessarily requires so much Attention, and the Public is disposed to give so little, that I shall still doubt for some time of its being at first very popular: But it has Depth and Solidity and Acuteness, and is so much illustrated by curious Facts, that it must at last take the public Attention. (C 186)

Hume and Smith had long been the closest of friends. Smith admired Hume more than anyone else in the world. He had learned from Hume in philosophy, in economics, and perhaps above all in thought about religion, though he was not prepared to be as outspoken as Hume on the subject. He regarded Hume as the greatest philosopher of the age and, while he differed in some points of moral theory, he thought that Hume's personal character and conduct exemplified moral goodness to perfection.

Hume had only a few months more to live when the *Wealth of Nations* appeared in the spring of 1776. He had been steadily declining as the result of a disease in the stomach and he died on 25 August. He was particularly anxious that his *Dialogues on Natural Religion* should be published immediately after his death and he had great difficulty in trying to persuade Smith to accept responsibility for seeing the book through the press. Smith's reluctance arose, I think, not simply, or even not so much, from apprehension of unpleasant consequences for himself, but more from a genuine belief that the *odium theologicum* would tarnish Hume's own reputation. In the event Smith was assailed for something different. Hume had written a short autobiography to be published after he was gone. Smith was so impressed with Hume's courage and good humour in the face of death that he resolved to add to the autobiography a brief account of Hume's last days, including an irreverently witty tale, inspired by a reading of Lucian's *Dialogues of the Dead*, about a conversation that Hume might have had with Charon, the ferryman who, in classical mythology, rowed the souls of the dead over the river Styx. Smith ended his account with a sentence imitating Plato's estimate of Socrates at the close of *his* account of the death of his mentor. Smith wrote that he had always considered Hume 'as approaching as nearly to the idea of a perfectly wise and virtuous man, as perhaps the nature of human frailty will permit' (C 221). Conventional Christians were shocked. How could an atheist be perfectly virtuous? Smith himself, they said, was promoting atheism by suggesting, through the example of Hume, that it afforded a protection against the fear of death. Smith reflected ruefully in a letter:

A single, and as, I thought a very harmless Sheet of paper,

25

which I happened to Write concerning the death of our late friend Mr Hume, brought upon me ten times more abuse than the very violent attack I had made upon the whole commercial system of Great Britain. (C 251)

In 1777 Smith applied for and was readily granted an appointment as Commissioner of Customs in Edinburgh. It brought him an income of £600 a year and he thought that he should now give up the annual pension of £300 from the Duke of Buccleuch. The Duke, however, insisted that the pension had been promised unconditionally and must continue. So Smith spent his last years in Edinburgh a comparatively rich man. (He in fact gave away a good deal of his wealth to charitable causes in secret.) He took a fine house in the Canongate and brought his mother and his cousin, Janet Douglas, over from Kirkcaldy to join him. A little later he also brought into his household a nephew of Janet's, David Douglas, whom he eventually made his heir. The Board of Commissioners of Customs met on four days a week for most of the year, and Smith attended its meetings with great regularity apart from a brief visit to London in 1782 and a more extended one in 1787. The company of his friends meant much to him. He kept open house for them at Sunday supper, and on Fridays he dined at the Oyster Club, founded by him and two distinguished scientists, Joseph Black and James Hutton, who were later to be appointed his literary executors. The name of their club seems to suggest that they were gourmets, but as it happens all three were more interested in conversation than in food and drink. Black was a vegetarian, Hutton a teetotaller, and Smith more fond of sugar lumps than anything else. At his Sunday supper parties Miss Douglas would place the sugar-bowl on her lap after a time in order to halt his raids upon it.

During Smith's visit to London in 1787 he saw a good deal of the younger Pitt, a warm admirer of the *Wealth of Nations* and a fervent advocate of Smith's free-trade principles. It is said that on the first occasion when they met, the company stood up at Smith's arrival, and upon his asking them to be seated, Pitt replied on their behalf: 'No, we will stand till you are first seated, for we are all your scholars.' Smith for his part came to reciprocate the admiration as he got to know Pitt better. There is another story that at a dinner party attended by both of them Smith said to a companion: 'What an extraordinary man Pitt is; he understands my ideas better than I do myself.'

Pitt may have appreciated the *Wealth of Nations* more than most, but it had exerted practical influence on others too, beginning with Lord North's introduction, in his Budgets of 1777 and 1778, of new forms of taxation recommended by Adam Smith, and continuing with consultation of Smith by members of the Government in 1778 on policy towards America and in 1779 on the proposal to grant free trade to Ireland. The book itself was republished in a second revised edition in 1778, considerably expanded in the third edition of 1784, and then reprinted in two further editions of 1786 and 1789. Meanwhile it had been translated into German, French (in three different versions), Danish, and Italian.

Towards the end of his life Smith spent many months on producing an enlarged version his first book, *The Theory of Moral Sentiments*. He also talked of being engaged on two other works, one 'a sort of philosophical history' of literature and 'philosophy' (no doubt including the sciences within that term), the other 'a sort of theory and history of law and government' (C 287). He said that he already had most of the materials and had made some headway with the actual writing. However, he never finished these books, and a week before his death he asked Black and Hutton to burn all his manuscripts, sixteen volumes of them, except for the few pieces which were later published as *Essays on Philosophical Subjects*. These, taken together with the report of his lectures on rhetoric and *belles-lettres* in 1762-3, give some indication of what the first of the two projected books might have been, just as the reports of his lectures on jurisprudence afford some evidence for the second. But when one compares the latter part of the jurisprudence lectures with the *Wealth of Nations*, one can see that the actual books, if Smith had brought them to fruition, would have been far superior to the initial writings from which they were to grow.

Adam Smith died in 1790 at the age of sixty-seven. He is buried in the Canongate churchyard, not far from the house in Edinburgh where he had lived for twelve years. His grave is at the foot of a simple monument with the following inscription:

Here
are deposited
the remains of
ADAM SMITH,
author
of the
Theory of Moral Sentiments,
and
Wealth of Nations;
&cc   &cc   &cc
He was born, 5th June, 1723.
And he died, 17th July, 1790.

3 Ethics

The first chapter of the *Moral Sentiments* is entitled 'Of Sympathy'; the first chapter of the *Wealth of Nations* is entitled 'Of the Division of Labour'. In each case the title is a signal of what Smith thinks most fundamental. The main subject of the *Moral Sentiments* is the nature of moral judgement and Smith founds it on sympathy. The main subject of the *Wealth of Nations* is economic growth and Smith founds that on the division of labour.

Sympathy

It is a mistake to suppose, as a number of nineteenth-century commentators did, that Adam Smith's first book treats sympathy as the motive of moral action. The role of sympathy in his book is to explain the origin and the nature of moral judgement, of approval and disapproval. For this purpose he uses the word 'sympathy' in a somewhat unusual way to mean not just sharing the feelings of another, but being aware that one shares the feelings of another. As often happens when a philosopher takes a term of common usage and employs it in a special sense, he sometimes forgets his own prescription and slips back into the normal meaning, but in general Smith is clear enough about what he is doing.

He uses his notion of sympathy to explain two different kinds of moral judgement or approval. The first is a judgement about the 'propriety' of an action; in plain language, the judgement that an action is right or wrong. The second is a judgement about an action's merit or demerit, the judgement that it deserves praise or blame, reward or punishment. According to Smith, the feeling of approval which is expressed in a judgement of right or wrong is the result of sympathy with the agent's motive. We can illustrate what he means with a simple example. If I see Alma Goodheart help a lame old lady across the road, I 'sympathize' with her kindness and as a result I approve of it as the appropriate response. I would have responded in the same way if I had been in her shoes and so I must think her response reasonable and proper. I say that her action was the right thing to do. A further judgement that the action is praiseworthy expresses a second form of approval, which arises from sympathy with the old lady's feeling of gratitude. On the other hand, if I see Ira Grumpy kicking a cat that has got in his way, I feel antipathy to Ira's annoyance and sympathy with the cat's resentment. The antipathy produces disapproval of the action as wrong, and the sympathy with resentment produces an additional and different disapproving judgement of the action as blameworthy.

When Smith says that an average spectator (he actually says 'every spectator' but that is rhetoric) would sympathize with the kindness of someone like my Alma Goodheart, he means that if the spectator imagines himself in Alma's shoes, he finds that he too would want to help the old lady; he observes a correspondence between the feeling, the prompting to action, which he would have and that which Alma evidently has. Likewise the spectator's 'sympathy' with the old lady's gratitude is a perception that, if he were in the old lady's situation and were helped, he would have the same feeling of gratitude that the old lady has. Antipathy towards an Ira Grumpy is an awareness, when you imagine yourself in his place, that you would not feel the same annoyance with the cat as he does. It will be seen that Smith's concept of sympathy is linked with the exercise of imagination. The sympathy that causes approval or disapproval is not necessarily awareness of an actual feeling which reproduces here and now the motives of those who act or the reactions of those whom the action affects. It is the thought of a feeling which you would have if you were in their shoes, an awareness that comes from imagining yourself in the situations of those who are actually involved.

The two judgements of approval that arise from sympathy are clearly rational, in Smith's view. A spectator who finds that the feelings of those involved correspond to what his own would be, must regard those feelings as appropriate to the situation.

> The man who resents the injuries that have been done to me, and observes that I resent them precisely as he does, necessarily approves of my resentment. The man whose sympathy keeps time to my grief, cannot but admit the reasonableness of my sorrow. He who admires the same poem, or the same picture, and admires them exactly as I do, must surely allow the justness of my admiration. (M 16)

Sympathy creates a social bond. This is plainly true of sympathy in its most common meaning of compassion; when one feels compassion for the sorrow or the need of another, one is moved to give comfort or help. Sympathy of this kind, serving as a motive of action, promotes a sense of responsibility to share the burdens of others. Sympathy in Adam Smith's sense is a socializing agent in a different way. Everyone, or nearly everyone, is pleased with the approval of others and uncomfortable with disapproval. I learn from experience that spectators approve when my feelings and reactions correspond to the feelings and reactions which they would have in my situation. If my natural reactions differ from the common norm, I shall meet with disapproval. So I have an inducement to conform, in order to win approval. If, for example, my natural reaction to sorrow or to injury is more vigorous than that of the average spectator, I am taught by his lack of approval to try to tone it down in future.

Such differences in sentiment between the observer and the person observed may arise from differences in the natural constitution of particular individuals. They are, however, also inherent in the process of imaginative sympathy. For all that the imagination allows us, in a sense, to identify ourselves with other people, imagining is not the same as actually experiencing, and the reproduction of feeling cannot match up to the original.

> The person principally concerned is sensible of this, and at the same time passionately desires a more complete sympathy. . . . But he can only hope to obtain this by lowering his passion to that pitch, in which the spectators are capable of going along with him. . . . What they feel, will, indeed, always be, in some respects, different from what he feels . . . These two sentiments, however, may, it is evident, have such a correspondence with one another, as is sufficient for the harmony of society. Though they will never be unisons, they may be concords, and this is all that is wanted or required. (M 22)

The spectator for his part is also aware that his feelings must fall short of those experienced by 'the person principally concerned'. The spectator too is influenced by the socializing tendencies of sympathy; he too would like to see a more complete concordance of feelings. So he strives to heighten his reaction by a closer identification, trying to take into his imaginative leap all the little details that make an experience more poignant.

These two efforts, on the one side to damp down the violence of experienced feeling, on the other to enliven the weakness of imagined reproduction, produce two different kinds of virtue, the virtue of self-command and the virtue of 'indulgent humanity' or sensibility. Smith's own ethical doctrine (as contrasted with his contribution to ethical theory) emphasized the value of self-command. It was at the forefront of Stoic ethics, which had impressed him deeply in his early years, especially from his reading of Epictetus. Epictetus was a Greek slave in the time of the Roman Empire, who became emancipated but whose earlier period of slavery had taught him to face the harsh burdens of life with fortitude, with what we would now call the 'stoic' virtue of resignation. One can see from the *Moral Sentiments* that Adam Smith was fascinated by Stoic ethics, although he came to see that certain features of the Stoic doctrine were unacceptable. Even so, his own code of ethics is more Stoic than Christian. He thought of himself as putting the two together. 'As to love our neighbour as we love ourselves is the great law of Christianity, so it is the great precept of nature to love ourselves only as we love our neighbour, or what comes to the same thing, as our neighbour is capable of loving us' (M 25).

The impartial spectator

So far I have been dealing with Smith's theory of the moral judgements which we make as spectators of the behaviour and character of other people. What of judgements about ourselves? Smith's answer to this question constitutes the most original and the subtlest part of his ethical theory. According to Smith, I approve or disapprove of my own actions by imagining myself in the shoes of a spectator. Let us go back to my earlier example of judging another person's action to be wrong. Suppose that I, like Ira Grumpy, were annoyed by a cat and were tempted to kick it, but said to myself 'No, that would be wrong.' Smith thinks that my moral disapproval is the result of the disapproval of spectators. I know that most people disapprove of such actions. Obviously they would disapprove of me just as much as they disapprove of Ira Grumpy. If I were somebody else and looked at myself kicking the cat, I should feel the same antipathy as I feel towards Ira. The judgements of conscience, moral judgements about one's own actions, are in the first instance a reflection of the judgements of society. Smith himself uses the image of a mirror.

Were it possible that a human creature could grow up to manhood in some solitary place, without any communication with his own species, he could no more think of his own character, of the propriety or demerit of his own sentiments and conduct, of the beauty or deformity of his own mind, than of the beauty or deformity of his own face. All these are objects which he cannot easily see . . . and with regard to which he is provided with no mirror which can present them to his view. Bring him into society, and he is immediately provided with the mirror which he wanted before. (M 110)

We suppose ourselves the spectators of our own behaviour, and endeavour to imagine what effect it would, in this light, produce upon us. This is the only looking-glass by which we can, in some measure, with the eyes of other people, scrutinize the propriety of our own conduct. (M 112)

If Smith had stopped there, his theory would be too simple. Spectators can make mistakes; they may be unaware of some of the facts or may misunderstand motives. A man's conscience sometimes tells him that he must go against popular sentiment. This, Smith thinks, is because he is in a better position than spectators to know the relevant facts. Of course, he too may misinterpret facts from partiality to his own interest, and this is why he should try to look at them in the guise of an impartial spectator. In order to avoid self-deceit we must try to see 'ourselves in the light in which others see us, or in which they would see us if they knew all' (M 158-9). It remains true, however, that we may think the judgement of actual spectators to be misguided through ignorance of some of the relevant facts. Even so, says Smith, we reach our moral judgement by imagining ourselves as an ideal impartial spectator, a spectator who knows all the relevant facts but is not personally involved. If we find that this imagined impartial spectator, 'the man within the breast', would sympathize with what we plan to do, or with what we have done, that causes us to approve. If the impartial spectator does not sympathize, we disapprove.

The late Professor A. L. Macfie observed that Robert Burns, who knew and valued *The Theory of Moral Sentiments*, probably had in mind Smith's phrase, 'if we saw ourselves as others see us', when he wrote

> O wad some Pow'r the giftie gie us
> To see oursels as others see us.

The touch of religious language in that couplet is also to be found in Smith's account of the impartial spectator. Smith most commonly writes of 'nature' as the source of our moral and other capacities but at times he is prepared to use theological language.

> The all-wise Author of Nature has, in this manner, taught man to respect the sentiments and judgments of his brethren . . . He has made man, if I may say so, the immediate judge of mankind; and has, in this respect, as in many others, created him after his own image, and appointed him his vicegerent upon earth, to superintend the behaviour of his brethren. (M 128-30)

The association with biblical ideas and phrases does not mean that Smith has abandoned explanation in terms of human nature, what we nowadays call empirical psychology. There is a fair amount of evidence, including some in the *Moral Sentiments* itself, that he had reservations about accepting Christianity, though he did not carry religious scepticism as far as Hume did. Smith was probably a deist. Like a number of other thinkers of the Enlightenment, he considered that observable nature afforded sufficient reason for believing in the existence of God. Smith's account of natural processes can be read as a would-be scientific enterprise, with no need for an underpinning from theology. In his ethics, as in his economics, scientific explanation was what he was after. However, both for Smith himself and for most of his readers an account of natural process was more persuasive, as well as more vivid, if nature were personified or treated as the work of a personal God. The metaphor of legal language, when he speaks of man as the judge of mankind, serves the same purpose. Sympathy and antipathy, with consequent approval and disapproval, take place as a matter of course. Spectators do not set themselves up to imitate earthly judges in courts of law, still less to imitate a heavenly judge. But the effect of their behaviour is analogous to that of intentional judges. Its significance is brought out by the comparison with judges and by the traditional language about God.

In the same spirit Smith is ready to say that the general rules of morality are 'justly' regarded as laws of God. They come to us from experience. Having found that our sympathy and consequent approbation tend to be directed upon the same sort of object on different occasions, we generalize our experience into rules or principles: for example, that it is right to help people in need, wrong to harm those who have intended no harm to us, right to reward the beneficent and to punish the evil-doer. It is equally natural for men to ascribe to their gods those feelings which matter most for the conduct of human life; since moral rules resemble laws, they are treated as divine laws attended by divine sanctions. The natural tendency is refined and confirmed by 'philosophical researches', which lead to monotheistic belief and which also observe 'badges of authority' in moral judgement; these badges or marks of authority are signs that moral judgement was intended by God to direct our lives. The last part of this argument (M 165) echoes an earlier moralist of the eighteenth century, Bishop Butler, who influenced the mature thought of Smith's teacher, Hutcheson.

Smith's moral psychology

Smith's theory is primarily an explanation of the origin of moral judgement, something that nowadays would be assigned to psychology rather than philosophy. The eighteenth century did not distinguish between the two disciplines, and for Adam Smith, as for Hume, psychological explanation was the most fruitful method of dealing with philosophical problems. In consequence Smith's theory about the psychology of moral judgement tended to determine his views on the philosophical problem of the standard of right action. The problem is to find a principle or set of principles for deciding what is the right thing to do. One answer that has immediate attractions is the view of utilitarianism: the proper standard is maximum promotion of the general happiness. Utilitarianism received its name from Jeremy Bentham but its substance was prominent enough earlier in the eighteenth century, and Adam Smith was well aware of its appeal. He was prepared to allow that moral actions do in fact tend, as a whole, to promote the general happiness, and that this is the end intended by God, but he opposed the view that utility is the one and only standard of right action. In practice, he argued, the thought of utility has a subordinate role in the formation of moral judgement. Our approval arises first from sympathy with the motive of the agent and secondly from sympathy with the gratitude of the beneficiary. Thirdly it receives added support from noting that the action conforms to the general rules of morality (which in fact, as he has explained, have their origin in the two kinds of sympathy). Then fourthly it may gain further confirmation from the pleasure which attends the thought of utility. According to Smith, the last consideration is also the least in its contribution to the final judgement of approval.

Smith's objection to utilitarianism is that we do not in practice decide what is right by reference to utility. Now if the problem of the standard of ethics were one of positive psychology, finding out how we do in fact reach our decisions, the objection would be conclusive. But the problem is a normative one; it is concerned with the question 'How *should* we decide?' Smith would still say, however, that the answer is to be gleaned from actual practice. Even if social utility is the ultimate end, nature achieves that end through the workings of sympathy. Defending his view that the concept of ill desert depends on sympathy with resentment, Smith writes:

> . . . the present inquiry is not concerning a matter of right, if I may say so, but concerning a matter of fact. We are not at present examining upon what principles a perfect being would approve of the punishment of bad actions; but upon what principles so weak and imperfect a creature as man actually and in fact approves of it. . . . Though man . . . be naturally endowed with a desire of the welfare and preservation of society, yet the Author of nature has not entrusted it to his reason to find out that a certain application of punishments is the proper means of attaining this end; but has endowed him with an immediate and instinctive approbation of that very application which is most proper to attain it. The oeconomy of nature is in this respect exactly of a piece with what it is upon many other occasions. (M 77)

The trouble with Smith's method of distinguishing between right and fact is that it ignores the practical problems which often face imperfect men in reaching moral decisions. In a dilemma, with the need to choose between competing goods (or evils), 'immediate and instinctive approbation' fails us. It is then that we want to ask the normative question 'How *should* we decide?'

If you were to ask Smith what is the standard of moral judgement, the criterion whereby you can decide what you ought to do, Smith would say it is the approval of the impartial spectator. That, however, will only tell you whether or not the impartial spectator has the same attitude to a proposed action as you have yourself. If your attitude is hesitation between conflicting goods, each of them affording some valid ground for choice, it does not help to know that the impartial spectator sympathizes. The function of the impartial spectator is to enable you to be impartial; if your initial inclination if affected by partiality, by a concern for your own personal interest, the impartial spectator will help you to take a more objective view. If, however, you have rid yourself of partiality but are still unclear about the respective merits of competing alternatives, the impartial spectator cannot help.

Nevertheless, as a psychological account of the origin of conscience the theory of the impartial spectator is impressive, especially in linking the moral judgements of the individual with those of society. The first stage of Smith's theory, his account of the approval of actual spectators, has a weakness. He says that the approval of a spectator is the result of awareness that he would share the agent's feelings if he were in the same situation. This does not distinguish between moral and other kinds of approval. When introducing his theory that approval depends on sympathy (in the sense of observation of correspondence), Smith himself gives a variety of examples to show that a judgement of propriety need not be a moral judgement.

The man whose sympathy keeps time to my grief, cannot but admit the reasonableness of my sorrow. He who admires the same poem, or the same picture, and admires them exactly as I do, must surely allow the justness of my admiration. He who laughs at the same joke, and laughs along with me, cannot well deny the propriety of my laughter. . . . If the same arguments which convince you convince me likewise, I necessarily approve of your conviction. (M 16-17)

Sympathy, the recognition of a correspondence, either of feelings or of opinions, produces approval. But what determines whether the approval, the judgement of propriety, is moral as contrasted with aesthetic or intellectual? Smith would say that moral approbation expresses sympathy with motives, but this seems too wide. Suppose I go to a concert from a desire to hear the music on the programme. A spectator who shares my tastes will approve of my action and its motive. Yet it would be distinctly odd to call his approbation moral.

However, this weakness in Smith's explanation of the judgement of propriety does not affect the value of his most important contribution to ethical theory, his concept of the impartial spectator. The approval of the imagined impartial spectator does indeed depend on Smith's earlier account of approval by actual spectators, so that it could apply to non-moral as well as moral approval; but this does not matter. Anyone who was bothered that his aesthetic tastes or his ambitions were unduly subjective could consult the judgement of an imagined impartial spectator. In practice such worries are concentrated upon moral issues, when we speak of an exercise of conscience. Even though Smith's concept of the impartial spectator could cover more than conscience, it can still be valuable as a psychological explanation of the latter.

Smith's explanation of the origin of conscience is in principle similar to that of Freud. Straightforward moral judgements about our own actions, according to Smith, are built up in the mind as a reflection of the attitudes of society, mediated especially in childhood through the influence of parents, teachers, and schoolfellows. The built-up set of attitudes in the mind acts as a second self passing judgement on the plans or actions of the natural self.

> When I endeavour to examine my own conduct, when I endeavour to pass sentence upon it, and either to approve or condemn it, it is evident that, in all such cases, I divide myself, as it were, into two persons . . . The first is the spectator, whose sentiments with regard to my own conduct I endeavour to enter into, by placing myself in his situation, and by considering how it would appear to me, when seen from that particular point of view. The second is the agent, the person whom I properly call myself, and of whose conduct, under the character of a spectator, I was endeavouring to form some opinion. (M 113)

Freud writes of a super-ego, a second self built up in the mind as a reflection, largely, of the attitude of parents, acquiring the function of a censor to pass judgement on the desires and actions of the natural self.

There are significant differences between the two theories. First, Freud places particular emphasis on the influence of parental attitudes, while Smith thinks more broadly of social norms and mentions teachers and schoolfellows as well as parents in inculcating these norms into the child. Secondly, Freud's super-ego seems to do much more in the way of disapproval than of positive approval. It includes an uplifting 'ego ideal' as well as a repressive 'conscience', but Freud emphasizes the latter element. The primary role of the super-ego is that of a censor, inhibiting the exuberance of sexual and associated impulses. Smith thinks of the impartial spectator as being there both to approve and to disapprove. There is no perceptible leaning to one side or the other. Thirdly, Smith adds the vital qualification that 'the man within the breast' can be a superior judge to 'the man without' in being better informed about facts and motives.

Psychoanalysts presumably find Freud's theory useful in their medical practice. One can well understand that certain types of neurosis are connected with an excessive sense of inhibition and that this is often the effect of an excessively censorious parent in childhood. If, however, Freud's theory is generalized and taken to be an explanation of the conscience of most normal people, then it seems less satisfactory than the explanation given by Adam Smith. Parents are no doubt the major influence in the moral education of children during their earliest years, but teachers and fellow-pupils, and then friends and fellow-workers, all have a part to play later on. A repressive family background can produce a rigid, censorious conscience, more inclined to 'don't' than 'do'; but an affectionate background at home and at school results in a more liberal conscience, encouraging both the development of self and a concern for others.

What of the third difference between Smith and Freud, Smith's readiness to make conscience a 'superior tribunal' to the judgement of actual spectators? Having had our eyes opened by Freud and others to the dark recesses of the unconscious, we may be inclined to treat Smith's view as a typical piece of eigheenth-century optimism, blind to the prevalence of self-deceit. That, however, is too simple-minded. Smith knew nothing of explicit theories of the unconscious but he was well aware of the strength of self-deceit.

This self-deceit, this fatal weakness of mankind, is the

43

source of half the disorders of human life. If we saw ourselves in the light in which others see us, or in which they would see us if they knew all, a reformation would generally be unavoidable. We could not otherwise endure the sight. (M 158-9)

Hence the need for the impartial spectator, to see ourselves as others see us – or rather, as 'they would see us if they knew all'. We do sometimes think that our own conscience is a better judge than popular opinion, and because of this it is a generally approved maxim that in such circumstances a person ought to follow the dictate of his own conscience. Smith tries to accommodate in his theory the facts of real life.

I have confined this account of Smith's ethics to his theory of moral judgement because that is the main topic of his first book and by far his most important contribution to moral philosophy. *The Theory of Moral Sentiments* has a good deal to say also about cardinal virtues. The earlier version of the book gave some prominence to the distinction between justice and beneficence, treating justice as primarily a negative virtue of avoiding harm to others, and beneficence as the positive virtue of doing them good. It balanced the Christian virtue of love, as the motive of beneficence, with the Stoic virtue of self-command, and it regarded prudence or rational self-interest as a proper object of approval, though not of warm admiration. The enlarged version of the book, put together some years after the publication of the *Wealth of Nations*, gives more prominence to prudence and also adds a little to the emphasis on self-command. This aspect of the *Moral Sentiments* invites comparison with the psychology underlying the *Wealth of Nations* and I shall say something in Chapter 5 about the comparisons that have been made.

The *Moral Sentiments* itself, however, has suffered from the preoccupation of scholars with these comparisons. It has been misunderstood, and its primary aim, as a work of moral philosophy, has been neglected.

4 Economics

The *Wealth of Nations* has two major features. The first is an analysis or (as present-day economists might say) a model of the workings of the economy. The second is a policy recommendation of free trade and *laissez-faire* generally. Both are connected with the underlying theme of economic growth. Adam Smith's analysis is not confined to showing the interrelation between the different elements of a continually maintained system. It also explains how the system can generate the continual accumulation of wealth. And since, according to Smith, this process is most successful when left to the play of natural forces, his analysis leads him to urge governments to let well alone.

The division of labour

Smith believes that the most significant aspect of economic life is the division of labour and he therefore begins his book with that topic. In Smith's view, the division of labour is the essential starting-point for economic growth, for the development of 'wealth' or 'opulence' in a society or in the wider world of international trade. In order to take this view he has to extend the idea of the division of labour to include technological advances, when new tools and new machines enable men to develop new specialized skills. Smith's suggestion is that concentration upon a single job or function makes it easier to think of improvements. He is well aware that many of the greatest improvements are due to engineers and manufacturers, but that comes later. Initially, he claims, it must have been the workers, the users of tools, who thought of ways to make their work easier; and this goes on all the time. Smith backs up the claim by a reference to experience.

page 9

> A great part of the machines made use of in those manufactures in which labour is most subdivided, were originally the inventions of common workmen, who, being each of them employed in some very simple operation, naturally turned their thoughts towards finding out easier and readier methods of performing it. Whoever has been much accustomed to visit such manufactures, must frequently have been shewn very pretty machines, which were the inventions of such workmen, in order to facilitate and quicken their own particular part of the work. (W 20)

In his Glasgow lectures he was more specific, showing that he had either himself visited a number of modern factories or had talked to people who had done so.

> The inventions of the mill or the plow are so old that no history gives any account of them. But if we go into the work house of any manufacturer in the new works at Sheffield, Manchester, or Birmingham, or even some towns in Scotland, and enquire concerning the machines, they will tell you that such or such an one was invented by some common workman. (J 351)

Smith introduces his discussion of the division of labour with a very simple example, the manufacture of pins. He takes a simple example because this makes it easy to see the essential point. Ten men working together in a small pin factory, sharing between them about eighteen simple operations, can make about 50,000 pins a day. If one man had to do all those operations by himself, and without the benefit of special machines, which are themselves the result of the division of labour, he could probably make little more than one pin a day.

Having illustrated the basic idea so clearly, Smith goes on to note the vast extent to which the division of labour affects the lives of all of us. Just look at the possessions of an ordinary working man, he says. The man's coat has been produced as a complex result of the work of a shepherd, a wool-sorter, a wool-comber, a dyer, a spinner, a weaver, and so on. Then merchants and sailors have been involved in transporting some of the materials used by certain of these workers. The same sort of long tale could be told about the production of the man's shoes, his food, his furniture, his household utensils. Then the chapter, the first chapter of the *Wealth of Nations*, ends like this:

> if we examine, I say, all these things, and consider what a variety of labour is employed about each of them, we shall be sensible that without the assistance and co-operation of many thousands, the very meanest person in a civilized country could not be provided, even according to, what we very falsely imagine, the easy and simple manner in which he is commonly accommodated. Compared, indeed, with the more extravagant luxury of the great, his accommodation must no doubt appear extremely simple and easy; and yet it may be true, perhaps, that the accommodation of an European prince does not always so much exceed that of an industrious and frugal peasant, as the accommodation of the latter exceeds that of many an African king, the absolute master of the lives and liberties of ten thousand naked savages. (W 23-4)

It is a splendid flourish with which to end an illuminating discussion, typical of the gifts of style which Adam Smith could summon up when necessary to drive home a point. Consider now just what the point is. First and foremost, of course, it is to show us how far economic growth, using the division of labour, has gone in developed societies as contrasted with static tribal societies. But it also shows us how far the inhabitants of a developed society depend on each other. The European peasant, unlike the African chief, has political power over nobody; yet his standard of life depends on the co-operation of perhaps as many people as are ruled by the tribal chief. The co-operation is neither commanded by a sovereign nor planned by the participants. It is nevertheless a firm sociological fact. Mutual dependence is, almost as much as economic growth, an underlying theme of Smith's analysis.

The dependence owes little or nothing to altruistic attitudes. A sociological study of the family or of religious communities or even of political society would have to take some note of those; but not a study of the economy. The benefits of the division of labour, says Smith, stem from simple self-interest in the practice of exchange.

> But man has almost constant occasion for the help of his brethren, and it is in vain for him to expect it from their benevolence only. He will be more likely to prevail if he can interest their self-love in his favour, and shew them that it is for their own advantage to do for him what he requires of them. . . . It is not from the benevolence of the butcher, the brewer, or the baker, that we expect our dinner, but from their regard to their own interest. (W 26-7)

Of course, the social benefits do not come from self-interest alone but from the effects of self-interest in the practice of exchange and before long in the conditions of a market. Smith attributes the practice of exchange to a 'propensity to truck, barter, and exchange one thing for another', and he shows curiously little interest in connecting this trait with his basic psychological and sociological analysis. He says it might be 'one of those original principles in human nature, of which no further account can be given', or it might be, 'as seems more probable', an outcome of 'the faculties of reason and speech' (W 25). His lectures at Glasgow indicate that by the latter phrase Smith has in mind 'the natural inclination every one has to persuade'. Offering a shilling, he says there, 'is in reality offering an argument' to persuade someone that it is in his interest to do as you suggest (J 352). Smith must have realized that this itself is not exactly a persuasive argument and so left it out of the *Wealth of Nations*. However, for the purposes of the economic analysis what matters is the result, not the original cause, of the practice of exchange. Exchange leads to a market and it is the laws of the working of the market that Smith wants to discover.

#3 One discovery which Smith believed he had made was that the division of labour is limited by the extent of the market. The stimulus for the division and subdivision of labour is the opportunity to exchange products or services. If other people are ready to exchange some of the corn and meat which they produce for the shoes which I make, I have an incentive to specialize in making shoes so as to sell most of them, instead of spending part of my time on making shoes (for myself and my family) and part on growing corn and grazing cattle. In a large town there is more opportunity for exchange, a larger market, than in a small village; and that is why you will find in the town but not in the village a high degree of specialization. In the town carpentry, joinery, cabinet-making, wood-carving are separate occupations of different skilled men; in the village one man will turn his hand to all of them as occasion arises.

The size of a market does not depend simply on the number of people who live in a particular area. It depends also on ease of communication with potential buyers and sellers elsewhere. Improvements in the transport of goods extend the market for them. Smith noted that (in his time) transport by water was much cheaper than transport by land. Economic historians tell us that he exaggerated the difference so far as the cost of transport within Britain was concerned, but the general point was perfectly valid, especially for international trade, and Smith rightly connected it with the way in which ancient civilizations and modern colonies developed first along sea coasts and river banks. In an earlier piece of writing on the topic he recalled an apt metaphor that could be applied more widely.

> What James the sixth of Scotland said of the county of Fife, of which the inland parts were at that time very ill while the sea coast was extremely well cultivated, that it was like a coarse woollen coat edged with gold lace, might still be said of the greater part of our North American colonies. (J 585)

If economic growth depends on the division of labour and if the degree of division of labour depends on the extent of the market, it follows that the continuation of economic growth requires an ever-widening market. This is one of the main reasons why Smith favoured free trade. He recognized, however, that the results of the whole process were not all welcome. The division of labour expanded material advantages but it also stunted the personality of many workers. The man who has to spend all his time on repetitive work, confined to a small number of simple operations, 'has no occasion to exert his understanding . . . and generally becomes as stupid and ignorant as it is possible for a human creature to become' (W 782). The rot spreads to his moral capacities, both domestic and civil, including his readiness to defend his country. In the Glasgow lectures Smith added that in England, where the division of labour had gone further than in Scotland, boys could get a paid job at the age of six or seven, had virtually no education, and when they grew up spent their leisure time in 'drunkenness and riot'.

> Accordingly we find that in the commercial parts of England, the tradesmen [i.e. the artisans] are for the most part in this despicable condition: their work thro' half the week is sufficient to maintain them, and thro' want of education they have no amusement for the other but riot and debauchery. So it may very justly be said that the people who cloath the whole world are in rags themselves. (J 540)

The remedy, Smith said in the *Wealth of Nations*, was for the public authority to provide elementary education in every parish. He even went so far as to suggest that it might be made compulsory. 'For a very small expence the publick can facilitate, can encourage, and can even impose upon almost the whole body of the people, the necessity of acquiring those most essential parts of education' (W 785). Adam Smith did not believe in *laissez-faire* for all aspects of social life.

The economic system

Exchange can be carried out by barter, with a valuation of

goods relative to each other. But this soon gives way to the use of some form of money, a non-perishable material, divided into standard units, which can serve as a generally accepted medium of exchange. Once money has been introduced, goods are priced in terms of it. Adam Smith draws a distinction between the 'real' price, or the value, of a commodity and its 'nominal' price or price in money. His account of value has given rise to much dispute and tends to obscure one's view of his account of 'nominal' or money price. It is the latter which is directly relevant to the working of the economic system. So let us put aside for the time being his theory of value and concentrate on (nominal or money) price.

The price that people are prepared to pay for a commodity depends on how much they want it. But the price that they are asked to pay depends not only on the demand but also on certain cost factors. Smith distinguishes three factors that may enter into the cost of a commodity: the wages of workers who have helped to produce it; the profit of the owners of 'stock' (capital in the form of money or of material things that are used in production); and the rent charged by the owners of land.

Smith goes out of his way to show that the three factors are different from each other. The profit of the farmer or factory owner is not a wage for his work of managing the enterprise. If it were, the amount of profit would vary with the amount of time, hardship, or ingenuity that was required by the work of management in a particular business; but in fact the amount of profit looked for by the owner varies with the amount of capital he has invested. Profit is a return on the investment of capital, which the owner could have used for other purposes, and which he risks losing in the enterprise to which he commits it. Rent on the other hand is different from profit as well as from wages. The landowner who charges a rent runs no risk of loss and has done no work for what he receives: 'landlords, like all other men, love to reap where they never sowed' (W 67), but unlike other men they are able to do so. 'They are the only one of the three orders whose revenue costs them neither labour nor care, but comes to them, as it were, of its own accord, and independent of any plan or project of their own' (W 265).

A few commodities may have nothing to do with rent and derive their cost from labour and profit alone; Smith gives the example of sea-fish, as contrasted with river-fish such as salmon, the taking of which involves a rent. Still fewer commodities, in a developed society, may have had only a labour cost with no element of profit for a provider of capital; Smith gives the example of certain coloured pebbles which were gathered from the sea-shore and sold by the gatherer to a stone-cutter. However, the price of most commodities has to include all three elements of cost. Corresponding to the three factors of cost are three economic groups, workers, providers of capital, and landowners, each of whom receives a portion of the cost of a commodity. They do not always have to be different individuals. A farmer might own his land, invest capital into using it, and join in the work of cultivation. Generally, however, the three functions are carried out by different people and an understanding of the economic system requires that they be distinguished.

Having done so, Smith next draws a distinction between 'natural price' and 'market price'. In principle his distinction is the same as that drawn later by Alfred Marshall between long-period and short-period price. Smith uses the term 'natural' because the long-period price is, in his opinion, the key to understanding a scientific law, a law of nature, about the working of the market. He more than once compares the natural price with a centre of gravity. 'The natural price, therefore, is, as it were, the central price, to which the prices of all commodities are continually gravitating' (W 75). Of course, it is not the natural price as such which exerts a quasi-gravitational force. The force is that of self-interest in the tension between supply and demand. However, the effect is an equilibrium which, Smith felt, could properly be compared with the equilibrium that the force of gravity can produce for moving bodies.

Smith in fact plays insufficient attention to the part played by demand. He recognizes it when writing of market price but he writes as if the natural price were determined solely by the three factors of cost. There is, he says, an average rate of wages, profit, and rent, depending partly on the general circumstances of a society (whether it is rich or poor; developing, stationary, or declining) and partly on circumstances peculiar to different occupations, enterprises, or pieces of land. The natural price of a commodity, according to Smith, is that price which just covers, no more and no less, the cost of production at average or 'natural' rates of wages, profit, and rent. The market price at any particular time can be at, above, or below the natural price and depends on the relation between supply and demand. (The relevant demand is 'effectual' demand, the demand of those who are able and willing to pay something like the natural price, the cost of making the commodity available for sale. A poor man would no doubt like to have a private carriage, but since he cannot afford to pay what it costs to produce such a carriage, his longing is not an effectual demand.) If demand exceeds supply, some people are prepared to pay more and the market price rises. If demand falls below supply, some goods are left unsold and dealers lower their prices in order to increase the demand and dispose of their stocks. However, any rise or fall in the market price above or below the natural price is bound to be temporary. When the market price is higher than the natural price, the prospect of a higher than average profit will induce more people to produce the commodity. The expanded supply, and competition between sellers, will reduce the market price. On the other hand, when the market price is lower than the natural price, the previous cost of production is not recouped. One or more of the three factors, wages, profits, and rent, will have to be reduced. The result of that will be that some workers will withdraw their labour and go off to another job; or some employers will reduce their use of capital for the production of these particular articles; or some landowners will refuse to let their land be used for the purpose connected with this particular production. So supply will fall, will be inadequate to meet the demand, and market price will rise. The general consequence is that the fluctuating market price must in time return to the natural price.

Since the natural price is in effect a semi-stable market price, to which other market prices tend to return, it is as much subject as they are to the influence of demand in relation to supply. Smith's own analysis shows that the average or natural rates of the cost factors, wages, profit, and rent, which are said to determine the natural price, are themselves subject to the play of supply and demand. The demand for labour, capital, and land from an enterprise producing one kind of commodity is in competition with demand for the same facilities from other enterprises producing other commodities; and the 'price' offered for these facilities, i.e. the rate of wages, profit, and rent, will depend on supply in relation to the competing demands. This is not to say that everything can be explained in terms of supply and demand. It is true, however, that Adam Smith's analysis should have been more explicit about the role of demand.

Smith does go on to show that the determination of wages, profit, and rent in the real world is a complex business that cannot be reduced to any single process like the play of supply and demand. He deals with each of the three factors of cost and is especially interesting on wages. Economists call this part of the work his theory of distribution, that is, his theory of how the money received for commodities is distributed among the three factors that make up the cost of production.

On wages Smith notes a conflicting set of determinants. Employers combine to keep wages low; workers try to combine to keep wages high. In this contest (at the time when Smith was writing) the employers had far the stronger position. There is, however, a basic minimum which must be paid, the cost of subsistence for the worker and his family, taking into account enough children (allowing for the early death of some) to replace him in due course. This sounds like a cold-blooded, purely economic consideration – the employer must not kill the goose that lays golden eggs for him – but Smith also speaks of the subsistence wage as 'the lowest which is consistent with common humanity' (W 86). Adam Smith the economist does not leave at home Adam Smith the moral philosopher.

However, workers are not always at the mercy of niggardly employers who have the power to keep wages down to a bare minimum. In a developing economy there is a demand for more labour, and employers are obliged to abandon their combination and to compete against each other in the hiring of workers, raising wages in the process. Smith illustrates the point by comparing the developing economies of Britain and America with the static

NB

economy of China and the declining one of Bengal. This leads him to the observation that 'It is not the actual greatness of national wealth, but its continual increase, which occasions a rise in the wages of labour' (W 87). He also notes that higher wages lead to a growth in population and in the health and energy of workers. The moral philosopher intervenes again in Smith's judgement on these consequences.

> Is this improvement in the circumstances of the lower ranks of the people to be regarded as an advantage or an inconveniency to the society? The answer seems at first sight abundantly plain. Servants, labourers and workmen of different kinds, make up the far greater part of every great political society. But what improves the circumstances of the greater part can never be regarded as an inconveniency to the whole. No society can surely be flourishing and happy, of which the far greater part of the members are poor and miserable. It is but equity, besides, that they who feed, cloath and lodge the whole body of the people, should have such a share of the produce of their own labour as to be themselves tolerably well fed, cloathed and lodged. (W 96)

In the absence of economic growth, wages would tend in the long run to decline to the subsistence level and that would be the 'natural' rate.

In addition to discussing the natural rate of wages, Smith tries to explain the difference in the rates of wages paid in different occupations. He gives five grounds of differentiation.

(1) Disagreeable work must command a higher wage than agreeable work if it is to attract enough workers to do it. One job can be more disagreeable than another

because the work is harder or dirtier or more dangerous or carries less status.

(2) Work which requires long or arduous training must have higher pay to recompense the cost or difficulty of that training. Smith compares training a man in a skill or a profession with creating an expensive machine. The cost of constructing the machine has to be recouped as part of the profit gained by its products, and it has to be recouped before the machine is worn out and replaced by another. Similarly the cost and difficulty (disagreeableness) of being trained for a skilled occupation or being educated for a profession is reflected in a higher wage or salary.

(3) Work which is irregular or insecure has to be paid more than that which is constant. For example, masons and bricklayers depend on the weather, coal-heavers depend on the arrival of ships bringing the coal to port.

(4) Occupations that carry a high degree of trust must carry a high wage. Smith gives two kinds of example. Goldsmiths and jewellers are entrusted with precious materials. Doctors and lawyers are entrusted with the health and the fortune or reputation of those who consult them. It is not clear, however, just what is common to these two kinds of trust so as to require higher pay in terms of Smith's account of the economic system. The higher pay for the goldsmith and jeweller is presumably a hedge against the temptation for them to steal the precious objects with which they are entrusted. The lawyer, entrusted with 'our fortune and sometimes our life and reputation' (W 122), is perhaps analogous in that he might manage to make off with our fortune; but why should he be tempted to risk our life or reputation? And why should the doctor be tempted to neglect our health? Smith says that the confidence we place in the doctor and lawyer 'could not safely be reposed in people of a very mean or low condition'

(W 122) and so we must enable the doctor and lawyer to have a high social status. I suppose his thought is that the doctor and lawyer must act in their professions with a high sense of responsibility to their clients, in short with a degree of altruism, unlike the butcher, the brewer, and the baker, who go about their business purely in a spirit of self-interest.

(5) Improbability of success, in the law for instance, has to be countered by the prospect of an especially rich reward if you are successful. This final ground for giving higher pay to some jobs than to others is substantially the same as the third, which postulated higher pay to compensate for insecurity (as well as irregularity).

In connection with his fifth ground Smith makes an interesting psychological observation. Men are prone, he says, to overrate their chances in the fortunes of life. They overrate the chances of gain and underrate the chances of loss. He cites the examples of lotteries and insurances. Since a lottery must bring some profit to those who run it, the overall chances of the punters must be less than the money they put in. Yet that does not deter people from having a fling in the hope of winning one of the glittering prizes. Many of them think that they will have a better chance if they buy several tickets, but on a strictly rational calculation they are simply increasing the probability of loss, since that probability advances towards the certainty of loss which comes from buying all the tickets, winning all the prizes, and losing the amount taken in profit by the organizers. Insurances illustrate the tendency of people to underrate the chances of loss. Many people neglect to take out insurance against fire, not because of a rational calculation of balancing the cost of the premium against the risk of loss, but simply because they imagine that the misfortune will not hit them.

This irrationality diminishes the effect of Smith's fifth ground for differentiating wages. As Smith himself observes, the psychological tendency to overrate one's chances of good fortune leads young men to disregard the risks of becoming a soldier or a sailor – or of entering professions such as the law. Smith notes that the pay for soldiers and sailors in his time was not greater than that for common labourers, although the risk element should have made it so. Likewise, in his opinion, while the fees of successful barristers seem high, the profession of law as a whole is underpaid in relation to the real chances of success or failure.

The general idea that comes out of Smith's account of wages is of an equilibrium between the unattractiveness of work and the attraction of monetary reward. Work has to be made worth while to those who undertake it. They will not accept a job if they can get the same pay for another job which is less unattractive or if they can get higher pay for another job which is no more unattractive. Smith is assuming that work in general is unattractive – 'toil and trouble'. The unattractiveness can take different forms: arduousness of the work itself or of the training for it, dangerous or unpleasantly dirty conditions, risk of failure. Where one kind of occupation is more unattractive than another, the attraction of a higher level of pay produces a balance. The inequalities of pay are offset by the counter inequalities in the degree of unattractiveness of occupations. Taking the advantages of pay together with the disadvantages of the relevant work, the inequalities disappear; or rather, they would disappear if there were no restraints on the natural economic process and if there were no limitations on the spread of relevant knowledge.

Smith's account of wages should also lead to the idea of an equilibrium between supply of and demand for labour;

but, as in his account of natural price, he does not draw attention to this. If the disadvantages of an occupation are not balanced by higher pay, the demand for workers in that occupation is not met and so employers have to increase the wage. On the other hand, if the monetary rewards of an occupation outweigh its disadvantages, it tends to be flooded with applicants for jobs and so the offered wages are reduced.

When he turns to average or natural rate of profit, Smith suggests that this can best be inferred from the average rate of interest, because interest and profit are alternative forms of return upon capital. Profit, like wages, is affected by economic growth or decline but in a reverse direction. A couple of the reasons for unequal wages also operate to produce unequal profits. A business which is disagreeable or has a low status, like keeping a tavern, brings a high rate of profit. So does an especially risky form of business, such as foreign trade – or smuggling! As with high wages for disagreeable or risky work, people are willing to take on the disadvantages of a disagreeable or risky business only if the disadvantages are balanced by especially high rewards.

The natural rate of rent, according to Smith, is the highest that a tenant can afford to pay, subject of course to the difference made by the fertility or situation of the land concerned. The price of products has to cover the ordinary cost of wages and the ordinary rate of profit. The surplus over and above these two elements is what the landowner demands as rent. Whether rent is high or low depends therefore on whether prices are high or low. Rent differs in this respect from wages and profits, the rate of which is a cause, not an effect, of the rate of prices.

Now that we have a picture of the relation of natural price to its three constituents, wages, profit, and rent, we can turn back to Smith's distinction between 'real' price or value and nominal or money price. Smith describes the first as the 'real measure' of exchangeable value.

> The real price of every thing, what every thing really costs to the man who wants to acquire it, is the toil and trouble of acquiring it. What every thing is really worth to the man who has acquired it, and who wants to dispose of it or exchange it for something else, is the toil and trouble which it can save to himself, and which it can impose upon other people. (W 47)

As we have seen in discussing different rates of wages for different occupations, Smith assumes that work, labour, is disagreeable; it is 'toil and trouble'. We undertake it for the sake of the useful things, the means to enjoyment, that it can bring. If we obtain goods, means to enjoyment, that have been produced by the labour of other people instead of our own, we are saved toil and trouble, and are prepared to pay for it. In a primitive state of society, a society of hunters, the only cost of acquiring goods is labour. In later stages of society the cost of profit and rent will be added. It remains true, however, that if I buy what others have produced I save myself toil and trouble, and that the purchase price represents a command over the toil and trouble taken by others instead of myself.

> The value of any commodity, therefore, to the person who possesses it, and who means not to use or consume it himself, but to exchange it for other commodities, is equal to the quantity of labour which it enables him to purchase or command. Labour, therefore, is the real measure of the exchangeable value of all commodities. (W 47)

However, it is often difficult to quantify labour in comparing the value of different things in relation to each other. One can quantify the amount of time spent on a piece of work, but time is not the only factor that counts in making work disagreeable. Work can be more or less arduous and can require more or less ingenuity (though it is not clear why Smith should assume that the exercise of ingenuity is disagreeable). In practice, values are settled 'by the higgling and bargaining of the market' (W 49), making allowance for hardship and ingenuity as well as time.

Smith prefaced his account of value and price with a plea for indulgence. The subject, he said, is 'in its own nature extremely abstracted' and might 'appear still in some degree obscure' after he had done his best to explain it (W 46). It has certainly left plenty of room for argument. Marx and others accused Smith of confusing the 'labour embodied' in a product with the 'labour commanded' by it, in trying to work out a labour theory of value. Modern economic theorists say that Smith's theory of value is concerned with quite a different matter, the problem of finding a measure or index of welfare, of the balance of 'utilities' (things that are wanted as being enjoyable or means to enjoyment) over 'disutilities'. Smith's prefatory remark shows that he was not clear about the relation between his account of value and that of money prices, but the charge of confusing 'labour embodied' with 'labour commanded' is certainly false. One can see why he tried to relate the 'disutility' (as modern economists call it) of toil and trouble to his theory of prices, but his account of the working of the economic system does not really need his theory of value.

Smith's analysis can apply to a static economy. The cost of producing goods is repaid by the distribution of the money earned to the three 'orders' of workers, employers, and landowners. Smith's main concern, however, is to explain economic progress, to show how a dynamic economy can generate a continual increase of wealth. Having learned from the physiocrats the general idea of representing the economy as the circulation of money and materials among the different groups, Smith went into much greater detail than they did in describing the functions of capital and income, the difference between fixed and circulating capital, the role of money and banks, and above all the importance of saving.

Smith points out that a man who does everything for himself, before there is a division of labour, can consume as he produces and does not need to keep a stock of goods. But once there is a division of labour and an exchange of the products of labour, a producer must keep the larger part of his products in stock against the time when they will be wanted by others. When they are sold, he uses part of the proceeds for his own immediate needs and part for the purchase of things (materials and tools) necessary to continue his production in the future. We may therefore divide his 'stock' (both of goods produced and of money received) into two parts, one for immediate consumption, the other for providing future income. The second part is capital and this itself is divided into two portions, circulating capital and fixed capital. Circulating capital is used for producing, buying, and selling, so as to make a profit; the money and the things that money buys circulate among producers, buyers, and sellers. Fixed capital is used for machines and tools, buildings, and the improvement of land; all these are means of production and they stay put, as contrasted with the money and goods that circulate.

As with the individual, Smith continues, so with the whole society. Its stock may be divided into a part which is reserved for immediate consumption or use, a part which consists in fixed capital, and a part which consists in circulating capital. However, when Smith applies his analysis to the economy of a country taken as a whole, its explanatory power becomes greater. The distinction between the categories is not necessarily the same as for an individual. For instance, a dwelling-house may bring revenue to a proprietor in the form of rent and so be part of his capital; but since the tenant has to pay the rent out of *his* revenue, the dwelling-house does not bring any additional revenue to society as a whole and so cannot be counted as capital but must be assigned to the stock reserved for consumption or use. Again, fixed capital for society at large includes the skills of the inhabitants – human capital – as well as the material means of production. Finally, the function of circulating capital is more complex and indeed central to the model of the economy. Here Smith is elaborating the idea of a circular flow which he had learned from Quesnay. Circulating capital consists of money and of goods (produced or in process of production) which will in due course be sold. Both money and goods circulate among the different groups of society. Money, obtained as wages, profit, or rent, is exchanged for goods, which eventually are withdrawn from the category of circulating capital, being transferred either to the stock of commodities reserved for immediate consumption or to that of fixed capital. The withdrawals need to be replaced by new production of raw materials or finished goods. Thus consumption and fixed capital both depend on circulating capital. Consumption so depends because nearly all goods for consumption are bought, not produced by the consumers. Fixed capital too depends on circulating capital, both when it is bought in the first place and when it is used to produce further goods.

The replenishment of circulating capital must come

from production, and we need to realize that only part of the labour force of society contributes to production. Many of the workers who provide services do not add to the value of production — servants, the armed forces, the public services, many of the professions, entertainers in the arts. Smith is not suggesting that these people are useless drones, like the idle rich. Their work is undoubtedly useful or (in the case of entertainers) pleasurable to society generally. Productive and unproductive labour both have value, but the value of productive labour is added to manufactured goods so as to be used later, while the value of unproductive labour is used up immediately.

> But the labour of the manufacturer [i.e. the worker engaged in manufacture] fixes and realizes itself in some particular subject or vendible commodity, which lasts for some time at least after that labour is past. It is, as it were, a certain quantity of labour stocked and stored up to be employed, if necessary, upon some other occasion. That subject, or what is the same thing, the price of that subject, can afterwards, if necessary, put into motion a quantity of labour equal to that which had originally produced it. The labour of the menial servant, on the contrary, does not fix or realize itself in any particular subject or vendible commodity. His services generally perish in the very instant of their performance, and seldom leave any trace or value behind them, for which an equal quantity of service could afterwards be procured. (W 330)

The same thing goes for other unproductive labour, including as it does 'some both of the gravest and most important, and some of the most frivolous professions'.

The labour of the meanest of these . . . and that of the noblest and most useful, produces nothing which could afterwards purchase or procure an equal quantity of labour. Like the declamation of the actor, the harangue of the orator, or the tune of the musician, the work of all of them perishes in the very instant of its production. (W 331)

Production can be increased either by increasing the number of productive workers or by improving their productive power with more and better machines or with more subdivision of labour. All these methods require additional capital, to pay for wages or machinery. The accumulation of capital depends on saving, on spending less in immediate consumption and using what is saved to increase production, either directly as an employer oneself or indirectly by lending the capital, for interest (a form of profit), to those who do undertake production. Saving is not leaving capital to lie idle but allowing it to be used productively instead of unproductively.

What is annually saved is as regularly consumed as what is annually spent, and nearly in the same time too; but it is consumed by a different set of people. That portion of his revenue which a rich man annually spends, is in most cases consumed by idle guests, and menial servants, who leave nothing behind them in return for their consumption. That portion which he annually saves, as for the sake of the profit it is immediately employed as a capital, is consumed in the same manner, and nearly in the same time too, but by a different set of people, by labourers, manufacturers, and artificers, who re-produce with a profit the value of their annual consumption. (W 337-8)

What is more, the savings of one year do not simply provide additional employment for one year. Since the additional labour produces goods that can more than pay its own cost, it can keep going in future years, so that the one lot of savings 'establishes as it were a perpetual fund for the maintenance of an equal number in all times to come'. When the benefits of saving are seen, additional savings are made available and wealth increases progressively. The circular flow of a static economy becomes a widening spiral movement in a growing economy.

It can just as well become a narrowing spiral movement in a declining economy, if excessive spending on immediate consumption leaves insufficient capital for maintaining the existing numbers of productive labour. Fortunately for human nature, the motive for saving is more pervasive than that for spending.

> the principle, which prompts to expence, is the passion for present enjoyment; which, though sometimes violent and very difficult to be restrained, is in general only momentary and occasional. But the principle which prompts to save, is the desire of bettering our condition, a desire which, though generally calm and dispassionate, comes with us from the womb, and never leaves us till we go into the grave. (W 341)

Natural liberty

It will be seen that the whole of this elaborate network of analysis depends on the motive force of self-interest, starting from entering into exchange, for easing toil and trouble, and ending with the accumulation of capital, for bettering our condition. The complex system, with its equilibria and its circular or spiral flows, owes nothing to deliberate planning. It exhibits a high and ever-increasing degree of mutual dependence, yet it all comes about naturally from the interplay of self-interest. In one section of the *Wealth of Nations* Smith uses a striking metaphor to reflect the paradox that a regard to self-interest can lead to the kind of universal benefit imagined by idealistic moralists and theologians.

> As every individual . . . endeavours as much as he can both to employ his capital in the support of domestick industry, and so to direct that industry that its produce may be of the greatest value; every individual necessarily labours to render the annual revenue of the society as great as he can. He generally, indeed, neither intends to promote the publick interest, nor knows how much he is promoting it. . . . he intends only his own gain, and he is in this, as in many other cases, led by an invisible hand to promote an end which was no part of his intention. (W 456)

Smith had previously used the image of the invisible hand even more colourfully in the *Moral Sentiments*. He there described the effects of economic growth in terms of employment.

> The earth by these labours of mankind has been obliged to redouble her natural fertility, and to maintain a greater multitude of inhabitants. It is to no purpose, that the proud and unfeeling landlord views his extensive fields, and without a thought for the wants of his brethren, in imagination consumes himself the whole harvest that grows upon them. The homely and vulgar proverb, that the eye is larger than the belly, never was more fully verified than with regard to him. The capacity of his stomach bears no proportion to the immensity of his desires, and will receive no more than that of the

meanest peasant. The rest he is obliged to distribute among those, who prepare, in the nicest manner, that little which he himself makes use of, among those who fit up the palace in which this little is to be consumed, among those who provide and keep in order all the different baubles and trinkets, which are employed in the oeconomy of greatness; all of whom thus derive from his luxury and caprice, that share of the necessaries of life, which they would in vain have expected from his humanity or his justice. . . . The rich . . . consume little more than the poor, and in spite of their natural selfishness and rapacity, though they mean only their own conveniency, though the sole end which they propose from the labours of all the thousands whom they employ, be the gratification of their own vain and insatiable desires, they divide with the poor the produce of all their improvements. They are led by an invisible hand to make nearly the same distribution of the necessaries of life, which would have been made, had the earth been divided into equal portions among all its inhabitants, and thus without intending it, without knowing it, advance the interest of the society, and afford means to the multiplication of the species. (M 184–5)

There is a significant difference between the two passages. The one in the *Wealth of Nations* says that the self-interested individual unintentionally helps to maximize the wealth of society. The one in the *Moral Sentiments* adds that he unintentionally helps to distribute it more widely, so as to approach equality. In writing this passage Smith had in mind Rousseau's *Discourse on the Origin of Inequality* and was implicitly contesting Rousseau's claim that the acquisition of property causes inequality. He probably had in mind also the opposed view of Bernard Mandeville, in *The Fable of the Bees: or Private Vices, Public Benefits*, that the so-called vices of luxury, pride, and fickleness were public benefits in spreading employment and increasing trade. Smith says that the poor obtain from the 'luxury and caprice' of the 'proud' landlord those necessities of life which they could not expect from 'his humanity or his justice'. Humanity or benevolence would seek to maximize the happiness of others; justice would seek to distribute it more equitably.

Adam Smith's image of the invisible hand is not a piece of theology. No doubt Smith would say that the beneficial results are ultimately due to nature or the divine author of nature, but he does not mean that a providential God pulls the strings all the time. He uses the phrase for vivid effect, to give us a picture of an imaginary controlling device, but he knows very well that the effect comes about automatically through the interplay of individual interest and the system of exchange. His perception of this truth is one of his great contributions to economic understanding.

Smith did not invent the phrase 'invisible hand'. It seems to have been an idiom of religious reflection. When the warship *Prince George* survived a great storm which wrecked several other ships of the Royal Navy in 1703, Flag Captain Martin wrote in the ship's log that 'the invisible hand of Providence relieved us'. In his early essay on the history of astronomy Smith wrote of pagan religion ascribing irregular events to 'the invisible hand of Jupiter'. He did not believe that the God of theism controlled the working of the economy any more than he believed that Jupiter controlled 'thunder and lightning, storms and sunshine' (P 49–50). He drew on the familiar heritage of religious language simply in order to make his readers appreciate the remarkable character of the phenomenon.

I do not mean that he deliberately placed a false halo around it. He was led by an invisible hand to choose evocative words.

No doubt Smith was predisposed to see a beneficent order in the natural running of human affairs. He probably acquired the idea from the ethical theory of the Stoics, which had impressed him deeply in his youth. Among other things, the Stoics believed in a cosmic harmony, which they described by the Greek word *sympatheia*, from which the modern word 'sympathy' is derived. They did not mean that all the elements in a harmonious universe literally had a fellow-feeling with each other. They meant that the elements all fitted in together, worked with each other in harmony. Adam Smith's use of the concept of sympathy in his ethical theory was individual to himself, but he often illustrates it by speaking of harmony, and I have little doubt that the Stoic notion of a harmonious system is at the back of his mind when he describes the socializing effect of our feelings of sympathy. It is likely that the same Stoic idea of a harmonious system helped him to think of the market as a system tending to the general benefit of society.

He did not, however, simply assume that the facts would conform to a preconceived idea. Adam Smith never approached his enquiries in that sort of spirit. He was an empiricist, a thinker who began with experienced fact and then produced a hypothesis to explain the facts. In economics he was impressed by the way in which the market can be observed to work, producing automatically reactions to changes in cost, supply, and demand so as to set up an equilibrium. His talk of market prices 'gravitating' towards the natural price shows that he was reminded of the system of mechanics, and the unplanned beneficial effects could have reminded him of the Stoic idea of a natural harmony.

This Stoic idea went along with a prescription to live according to nature and was one of the sources of the tradition of natural law. Smith was familiar with that tradition in the work of seventeenth-century jurists and philosophers, notably Grotius, Pufendorf, and Locke. He made his own signal contribution to it by interpreting normative or prescriptive natural law as arising from scientific laws of nature. That is to say, Smith treated general principles telling us how we ought to behave as being the result of general truths about the way people do in fact behave. Sympathy and the desire to have the good opinion of others cause people generally to be helpful to each other and to avoid doing harm; such behaviour is approved as the way we ought to act. Common self-interest leads to enforcing the most vital of such practices with the sanctions of criminal law. A similar common self-interest among states leads them to agree upon limited principles of international law. Likewise the practices of economic life, initiated by self-interest, have become established practices precisely because they are generally beneficial, although no one has planned the result. Because they are beneficial, they should be treated as prescriptive, the way we ought to behave.

The tradition of natural law included a belief in 'natural' liberty and equality. In a state of nature (an ambiguous expression which could mean either an unspoiled primitive condition or a utopian ideal) all human beings are free and equal. Adam Smith frequently writes of natural liberty but almost as frequently of natural justice and natural equality. Towards the end of Book IV of the *Wealth of Nations* there is a commonly quoted reference to 'the obvious and simple system of natural liberty' (W 687). Smith's earlier references to natural liberty, however, usually couple it with natural justice or equality or both. Even the passage which I have just quoted goes on to explain that natural liberty is limited by justice. 'Every man, as long as he does not violate the laws of justice, is left perfectly free to pursue his own interest his own way.'

As with natural harmony, the idea of natural liberty is a background conception which adds a unifying framework and gives scope for some persuasive rhetoric; but it is not the primary source of Smith's arguments for *laissez-faire*. His arguments are directed mainly at two particular targets and are based on solid empirical evidence about those two particular things. The first is restriction on competition and the mobility of labour; the second is restriction on the freedom of international trade. It should be noted, incidentally, that Smith attacks the first for producing unnatural 'inequalities' in the labour market, another indication of his view that natural liberty goes together with natural equality.

Under the first heading Smith criticizes the exclusive privileges of corporations which enabled them to retain outmoded practices on apprenticeship. The number of apprentices was limited and the period of their training was much longer than it need be. Consequently the supply of labour for skilled occupations was restricted. On the other hand, the endowment of scholarships and similar awards for education in certain professions, notably the ministry, unduly enlarged the supply of people entering them beyond the level which natural competition would produce. Then again, there were laws which unnecessarily restrained the movement of workers; the Statute of Apprenticeship more or less restricted people to one skilled trade, and the English Poor Law made it difficult for a poor man to obtain a 'settlement' (eligibility for relief) in a different parish from that of his birth.

Smith observed in another connection (laws of hereditary

succession) that 'Laws frequently continue in force long after the circumstances, which first gave occasion to them, and which could alone render them reasonable, are no more' (WN 383). Natural conservatism gets in the way of repealing obsolete laws which once were useful but which have come to be harmful. In this respect the natural tendencies of human behaviour are not beneficial and need the intervention of reforming legislation. So Smith's criticism of restrictive practices has its anti-libertarian aspect too.

When Smith turns, in Book IV of the *Wealth of Nations*, to freedom of international trade, he compares its advantages with those of exchange in a simple system of division of labour, and adds: 'What is prudence in the conduct of every private family, can scarce be folly in that of a great kingdom' (W 457). Free trade encourages countries to specialize in the kinds of production for which each has an advantage, and to benefit from exchange at cheap prices. This gives a country a greater total of desirable commodities than it would have if it produced everything for itself; for the latter policy would use up a larger proportion of the country's capital in producing the same amount of those goods that are imported cheaply under free trade. Smith's case is made, however, not with hazardous general statements of this kind, but with a detailed examination of the disadvantages of particular protectionist measures: bounties, duties, prohibitions of imports. He also adds reservations to the general case for free trade. First, he says, protectionist measures are justified in the interests of national defence, which is 'of much more importance than opulence' (W 465), and he gives as an example the introduction of the Navigation Act of 1651. Since the defence of Britain depended so much on ships and sailors, it was legitimate to give British shipping a preference in the carrying of goods. (Later in the book, however, when he came to discuss policy towards the American colonies, Smith was at pains to insist that in commercial terms the Navigation Acts were not beneficial.) Secondly, Smith approves of taxing imported goods if domestic goods of the same character are already taxed; otherwise there will not be fair competition. He also allows that there must often be a compromise with the principles of free trade in order to meet the circumstances of the real world: if a foreign country prohibits the importation of your goods, you may have to retaliate; when nearly every country limits freedom of trade in corn, it would be foolhardy for a small country to have no restrictions on the export of corn and so risk a famine. A general case for free trade must not blind us to realities. 'To expect, indeed, that the freedom of trade should ever be entirely restored in Great Britain, is as absurd as to expect that an Oceana or Utopia should ever be established in it' (W 471).

Laissez-faire in domestic policy is also subject to some limitation in Smith's proposals. He assigns three duties to the State: defence, the administration of justice, and the provision and maintenance of certain public works and institutions. He also has no objection to legal restriction on the rate of interest, although he does not prescribe this as a positive duty of the State. The first two of the three duties laid on the State would commonly be called political and not economic functions. Smith thinks of both in the traditional manner of libertarian thought; they are duties of protection. Defence is 'the duty of protecting the society from the violence and invasion of other independent societies'; the administration of justice is 'the duty of protecting, as far as possible, every member of the society from the injustice or oppression of every other member of it' (W 687). The third duty, however, goes beyond the traditional protective duties of what has been called the night-watchman State. This third duty requires the State to provide and maintain certain positive facilities for improving welfare. Smith's view is that the State should assume responsibility for those public works and institutions 'which it can never be for the interest of any individual, or small number of individuals, to erect and maintain; because the profit could never repay the expence' to them, though it may well do so to society as a whole (W 688). The public works which he has in mind are those necessary for commerce: roads, bridges, canals, harbours. When he turns to institutions, Smith thinks partly of commerce again and partly of education. Foreign trade requires protective forts in some countries and ambassadors in all. As for education, we have already seen that Smith believes the State has a duty to remedy the evil effects of the division of labour by encouraging or even 'imposing' elementary education upon all who would not acquire it privately.

Public responsibility for such works and institutions should, however, in Smith's view, be strictly limited to the areas where there would not be sufficient inducement for private enterprise. Moreover, even when facilities are publicly provided, the maintenance and running of them should call on the normal economic inducements for the sake of efficiency. Public works – roads, bridges, canals, harbours – should be made to pay for themselves, if this is possible, by means of tolls or port-duties. This method of financing them ensures that they will be constructed where they are needed and on the scale required by use; otherwise they might be planned merely to suit the convenience or caprice of some powerful individual. In the actual administration of tolls, sometimes private ownership is

more efficient, sometimes management by commissioners. For example, Smith says, there is a difference
between canals and roads. Canals will not be used unless
kept in good order; a private owner will therefore have an
incentive to look after them properly, while public
commissioners might be slack. On the other hand, roads
which are not kept in good repair can still be used, so private
ownership of the tolls will not ensure proper maintenance,
while public management will. It is not easy to see why
public management cannot be equally zealous about the
maintenance of canals, so the example is not convincing,
but one can appreciate the general point that private
ownership sometimes has an adequate incentive and
sometimes not. When Smith turns to education, he warmly
commends the practice, in the Scottish universities and
parish schools, of making the income of teachers come
partly from the fees of their pupils. This gives the teacher
a sense of dependency on the pupils and induces him to put
forth his best efforts. Where the teacher has a fixed stipend,
independent of the fees paid by students, he has no such
inducement; hence the slackness of the university teachers
at Oxford.

Adam Smith's faith in the virtues of natural liberty and
natural equality is overdone. He looks at them through
rose-tinted spectacles. The *Moral Sentiments* passage on
the invisible hand is extravagant in its picture of natural
equality. It says that the employment of the poor by the rich
produces an almost equal distribution of the necessaries of
life, and it then goes on to suggest that a near equality in
'real happiness' does not need employment anyway.

When Providence divided the earth among a few lordly
masters, it neither forgot nor abandoned those who
seemed to have been left out in the partition. These last

too enjoy their share of all that it produces. In what constitutes the real happiness of human life, they are in no respect inferior to those who would seem so much above them. In ease of body and peace of mind, all the different ranks of life are nearly upon a level, and the beggar, who suns himself by the side of the highway, possesses that security which kings are fighting for. (M 185)

This piece of romanticism may be influenced by the egalitarianism of Rousseau, whom Smith seems to have had in mind when he wrote the whole paragraph. A trace of the same sort of optimism remains in the *Wealth of Nations* when Smith argues that all occupations, if different degrees of reward are balanced against different degrees of toil and trouble, yield an equal amount of welfare.

When he comes down to particular proposals, however, Smith does not rely on a general faith in the prowess of nature. Instead he calls on the evidence of history to show that a practice has been harmful or beneficial, and he makes detailed recommendations in the light of that evidence. The rhetoric of natural liberty and natural equality is used to add persuasive effect but not as the core of his arguments.

Smith's political economy

Smith begins Book IV of the *Wealth of Nations* with a definition of 'political economy'.

Political oeconomy, considered as a branch of the science of a statesman or legislator, proposes two distinct objects; first, to provide a plentiful revenue or subsistence for the people, or more properly to enable them to provide such a revenue or subsistence for themselves; and secondly, to supply the state or commonwealth with a revenue sufficient for the publick services. It proposes to enrich both the people and the sovereign. (W 428)

What he has written previously meets the first of the two aims of the subject. Book IV itself is a survey 'Of Systems of political Oeconomy' alternative to his own. It is comparable to the survey, in Part VII of the *Moral Sentiments*, 'Of Systems of Moral Philosophy' prior to Smith's own theory. Both surveys illustrate Adam Smith's method of making headway in a subject. He examines and criticizes earlier theories in order to advance to a sounder theory. The programme is designed to enable him to learn from the earlier theories. Smith is happy to adopt from them what he regards as sound, and in rejecting what is unsound he is led to suggest a more viable alternative.

In the *Wealth of Nations* he considers two systems of political economy, that of the mercantilists and that of the physiocrats. His criticism of the mercantilists is severe and leads to his arguments for free trade. The basic fallacy of mercantilism is set out in the first words of Chapter I, 'That wealth consists in money, or in gold and silver', instead of goods. Smith has a much warmer opinion of the physiocrats, from whom he had learned a good deal and whose basic ideas of liberty and trusting nature were close to those with which he himself began. Their 'capital error', he believed, was to regard agriculture alone as productive while manufacture and trade were unproductive (W 674). Nevertheless he was prepared to go along with them in thinking that agriculture was the most productive element in the economy. The great virtue of the French economists was that they, like Smith, had perceived the fallacies of mercantilism. His conclusion on the physiocrats was as follows.

> This system, however, with all its imperfections is, perhaps, the nearest approximation to the truth that has yet been published upon the subject of political oeconomy . . . Though in representing the labour which is employed upon land as the only productive labour, the notions which it inculcates are perhaps too narrow and confined; yet in representing the wealth of nations as consisting, not in the unconsumable riches of money, but in the consumable goods annually reproduced by the labour of the society; and in representing perfect liberty as the only effectual expedient for rendering this annual reproduction the greatest possible, its doctrine seems to be in every respect as just as it is generous and liberal. (W 678)

The second of the two aims of political economy set out in Smith's definition of the subject requires a programme for taxation and other sources of public revenue. Book V of the *Wealth of Nations*, constituting well over a quarter of the whole work, is largely concerned with public finance, including proposals for raising revenue and a critical discussion of public debt. It also recognizes that the expenses required by the three duties of government raise special problems. The remuneration of members of the armed forces, of the people concerned with the administration of justice, and of those who maintain public works and public institutions (including teachers and the clergy) cannot be settled by the forces of the market. As is his wont, Smith faces these problems with a historical survey of different methods that have been tried.

When introducing the topic of taxation, Smith lays down

four general maxims. First, taxes should be levied in accordance with the ability of people to pay. Second, taxes should be certain and not arbitrary. That is to say, the taxpayer should know clearly beforehand how much tax he is liable to pay and when; it should not be left to the arbitrary judgement of the tax-gatherer. Third, the time and manner of payment should aim to suit the convenience of the taxpayer. Fourth, the levying of taxes should be as economical as possible. It should avoid the waste of unnecessarily large administration; it should not kill the goose by being a disincentive to industry or by ruining evaders with stiff penalties. Smith describes these maxims as having 'evident justice and utility'. So they have, but the fact was insufficiently appreciated in his time. Not that Smith is particularly original in formulating the maxims. His teacher, Hutcheson, had said much the same thing in a summary form, and so had Smith's contemporary, Sir James Steuart, whose *Principles of Political Oeconomy* was published in 1767. As in so much else, however, Adam Smith set out with especial clarity the relation of the relevant points to his system of political economy as a whole.

This indeed is the cardinal virtue of the *Wealth of Nations*. Not all readers have shared in the general admiration of the book, and the comments of one important scholar are worth noting at this point. J. A. Schumpeter, in his monumental *History of Economic Analysis* (1954), made a number of deprecatory remarks about the *Wealth of Nations* as a contribution to economic science: 'But no matter what he actually learned or failed to learn from predecessors, the fact is that the *Wealth of Nations* does not contain a single *analytic* idea, principle, or method that was entirely new in 1776.' Yet Schumpeter felt bound to allow that the *Wealth of Nations* 'is a great performance all the same' because of its 'co-ordination'. This was intended to be rather faint praise. The task of co-ordination required 'a methodical professor' and Smith 'was fitted for it by nature'.

Schumpeter underrates the character of Smith's systematization. Methodical co-ordination of the ideas of other people could not have produced a comprehensive system of the whole economic process, all parts of which interact with each other so as to maintain a self-adjusting balance and steady growth. Smith derived much of his material from other people but it needed imaginative vision to use that material as constructively as he did. Even Schumpeter is virtually obliged to contradict himself when he describes the first leading feature of Smith's book: 'Though, as we know, there is nothing original about it, one feature must be mentioned that has not received the attention it deserves: nobody, either before or after A. Smith, ever thought of putting such a burden upon division of labour.' Whether Smith was right or wrong to do so, it was a new idea if nobody else had thought of doing it. In fact this feature of the *Wealth of Nations* is simply one aspect of the imaginative vision which Smith applied to his materials in order to build a comprehensive system. We shall see later how it links up with his own view of the imagination needed for scientific work. It is an example of the way in which Smith's philosophical interests colour his scientific work.

Schumpeter could not have seen this since he believed that philosophy has nothing to contribute to economics; it simply gets in the way. For all his great learning, Schumpeter had his blind spots. While appreciating the 'intellectual stature' of Smith's *Essays on Philosophical Subjects*, especially the essay on the history of astronomy, Schumpeter says of them: 'were it not for the undeniable fact, nobody would credit the author of the *Wealth of Nations* with the power to write them.' The words 'nobody would' mean 'Schumpeter would not'. Those who read the *Wealth of Nations* with more sympathy and imagination than Schumpeter did can see that the philosopher who began the essay on the history of astronomy with a theory of scientific systems is himself applying that theory in his construction of an economic system.

5 Comparisons

Although Adam Smith must have taken great care to find the best words for his many memorable aphorisms, he did not take enough to guard against apparent inconsistencies in his work. I said at the beginning of Chapter 3 that Smith uses the term 'sympathy' in a special sense but is liable to slip back into the common usage of the word. His special sense is the perception that an imagined feeling in oneself would correspond with an observed feeling in someone else. Smith uses this concept to explain moral *judgement*, the approval or disapproval of actions. The common usage of 'sympathy' refers to the actual experience of fellow-feeling, especially fellow-feeling with distress. This can and often does act as a *motive* of action, a motive to give aid and comfort. It is not surprising that Smith should slip back into this common usage, but it is unfortunate that he should have done so in the context of the main reference to economics in the *Moral Sentiments*. The 'invisible hand' passage in that book says that the poor obtain from the self-interested behaviour of the rich man the necessaries of life which they could not expect from his 'humanity' or his justice. Continuing the theme, Smith writes that a patriot who exerts himself for the public weal is not always motivated by 'pure sympathy with the happiness of those who are to reap the benefit', that a man who encourages the repair of roads does not usually act from 'a fellow-feeling with carriers and waggoners', and that a legislature which protects the manufacture of cloth 'seldom proceeds from pure sympathy' with the wearer, still less with the manufacturer (M 185). The word 'sympathy' is twice used as a synonym for 'humanity' and 'fellow-feeling', all these terms serving to denote a motive of action.

Scholars who have concerned themselves with the interpretation of the *Wealth of Nations* have, naturally and rightly, turned to the *Moral Sentiments* as a source of further information. Naturally, too, they have concentrated on those parts of the *Moral Sentiments* which are directly relevant to Smith's views on economics. More often than not, they have just skimmed over the rest of the book, with no particular interest in, and perhaps no particular capacity for, understanding Smith's primary aim in writing the work. They have seen that an emphasis on sympathy pervades the whole book and they have observed that the term appears, in the main passage relevant to economics, as an altruistic motive of action. The reference to an invisible hand at once recalls the same phrase in the *Wealth of Nations*, and the statement that publicly beneficial actions do not proceed from 'sympathy' recalls the aphorism of the later book that we do not expect our dinner from the 'benevolence' of the butcher, brewer, and baker. In this 'economic' passage of the *Moral Sentiments* Smith appears to go along with the doctrine of the *Wealth of Nations* about beneficial action motivated by self-interest (though in fact he is talking about the aesthetic love of order rather than simple self-interest), but using the words 'sympathy', 'fellow-feeling', and 'humanity' in place of 'benevolence'. So far, so good.

However, some of these scholars found a problem in the fact that the *Moral Sentiments* as a whole gives so much prominence to the effect of sympathy in human life. Apart from the 'economic' passage, Smith writes as if sympathy played the major part in binding society together. How, then, these scholars asked, can this be reconciled with the view of the *Wealth of Nations*, which is surely that self-interest is the mainspring of social activity and that benevolence (or sympathy) counts for nothing? This was 'the Adam Smith problem', over which much ink was spilled in the nineteenth century, mainly by German scholars, though the English historian H. T. Buckle must share in the responsibility for misunderstanding. Adam Smith's own carelessness in his use of the term 'sympathy' was a contributory factor, but if the problem-mongers had taken the trouble to read and follow the whole of the *Moral Sentiments* they would not have gone so wildly wrong.

Their assumption was that in the *Moral Sentiments* Smith took sympathy to be the most influential of human motives, while in the *Wealth of Nations* he gave that role to self-interest. Carl G. A. Knies suggested in 1853 that Smith changed his mind as the result of his visit to France between the writing of the two books. H. T. Buckle in 1861 had a different explanation. Smith did not change his mind; he was dealing with 'two divisions of a single subject', 'the sympathetic' and the 'selfish' parts of human nature, a classification which was, in Buckle's opinion, 'a primary and exhaustive division of our motives to action'.

> In the *Moral Sentiments*, he ascribes our actions to sympathy; in his *Wealth of Nations*, he ascribes them to selfishness. A short view of these two works will prove the existence of this fundamental difference, and will enable us to perceive that each is supplementary to the other; so that, in order to understand either, it is necessary to study both.

Good advice, but Buckle had not taken it sufficiently to heart himself. He attached great importance to methodology and had some curious views about it. He had persuaded himself that all Scottish philosophers of the eighteenth century used deductive reasoning only and would have nothing to do with induction. Adam Smith, according to Buckle, went further still. He followed his own 'peculiar form of deduction', imitated from geometry, which required him to separate one set of premisses from another; and therefore he dealt with the two motives of sympathy and selfishness in two separate books. Buckle was presumably thinking of the fact that a theorem in geometry must confine its deductions to what follows strictly from its particular premisses. Adam Smith, in Buckle's view, began his first book with the premiss that a large class of human actions is motivated by sympathy and he was required by his method to confine himself to what is covered by that premiss; he began his second book with the premiss that the remaining class of human actions is motivated by selfishness and he had to confine himself in the second work to what is covered by that particular premiss.

This piece of fantasy was rejected by Witold von Skarżyński in 1878 on the ground that a device of logical method cannot remove inconsistency. Reverting to the view that Smith had changed his mind, Skarżyński then added his own fantasy that both of Smith's books were unoriginal anyway; the ethical theory was a botched repetition of Hume, and the economic was learned from the physiocrats. The report that Smith had included the substance of his economic doctrines in his Glasgow lectures on moral philosophy was dismissed by Skarżyński as incredible, all the more so since it included a story that these 'valuable lectures' (as Skarżyński ironically called them) were conveniently burned just before Smith's death.

The basic error lying behind all these interpretations is the supposition that Adam Smith in the *Moral Sentiments* gives sympathy a central role as a motive of action. In both books the influence of sympathy (or 'benevolence' or 'humanity') as a motive is very limited. In the *Moral Sentiments* the influence of sympathy as a binding social force of approbation is immense.

Although 'the Adam Smith problem' is a thing of the past, traces of it linger on. I do not think that anybody now says that the *Moral Sentiments* makes sympathy the predominant motive of human action in general, but one still finds able economists and historians of economic theory saying that Adam Smith regarded sympathy as the motive of morally virtuous action and self-interest as the motive of (non-moral, though not immoral) actions of economic life. In fact Smith explicitly criticizes his teacher Hutcheson for confining the motive of virtuous action to altruistic benevolence and for treating self-interest as a morally neutral motive. Smith himself thinks that rational self-interest (prudence) is a virtue from the moral as well as the economic point of view, though not one of the highest moral virtues except when it is infused with self-command, sacrificing immediate pleasure for long-term happiness. He certainly regards benevolence (or 'humanity', or 'sympathy' in the popular use of that word to denote a motive of action) as a more commendable moral virtue but he thinks that its effective occurrence is limited. He places rather more stress on other virtuous motives, self-command, the sense of duty (which he explains by his theory of the impartial spectator), and a regard to justice.

A different sort of contrast between the *Moral Sentiments* and the *Wealth of Nations* was made by the American scholar Jacob Viner in a widely praised article of 1927 called 'Adam Smith and Laissez Faire'. It is praised because it shows that Smith's support of *laissez-faire* is subject to substantial limitations and that his picture of the harmonious order of natural liberty includes a number of defects which 'would suffice to provide ammunition for several socialist orations'. Viner precedes these enlightening remarks by a review of the *Moral Sentiments* as containing a more idealized picture of the natural order which cannot be reconciled with the more mature and more realistic opinions expressed by an older Adam Smith in the *Wealth of Nations*.

He quotes at some length five passages from the *Moral Sentiments* as evidence for his view of that book. The first was in fact composed long after the *Wealth of Nations* for the enlarged version of the *Moral Sentiments*, published in 1790. It presents the idea of a benevolent God as one which has been held by many people and notably by the Stoic philosopher and Roman emperor, Marcus Aurelius. Smith says it is a helpful doctrine to those who believe it. He does not say it is true. The second passage would have been acceptable to virtually any pre-Darwinian scientist. It says that natural instincts tend to favour, more than anything else, self-preservation and the preservation of the species; it attributes these effects to an apparent intention in nature or the author of nature. The third passage is not at all idealistic. It says that the *economic* virtues of 'industry, prudence, and circumspection' commonly meet with 'success in every sort of business', with 'wealth and external honours' (M 166). This is hardly inconsistent with the *Wealth of Nations*. The passage is followed by a paragraph saying that our natural feelings would prefer to see moral virtues rewarded more than the economic virtue of industry, which can be possessed by a 'knave'. Viner detaches the subsequent passage and prints it as the last of his five quotations, presenting it as a 'concession' by Smith to the sad truth that nature can be unjust. The fact is that when the two passages are taken together, as they are given in Smith's book, they both show a fairly down-to-earth appraisal of the real world. Viner's remaining quotation, fourth on his list, is – inevitably – the invisible hand passage. This, as we have seen, does indeed end with a piece of romantic idealism about equality. It can be compared with the belief in the *Wealth of Nations* that the balance of toil and recompense is pretty well equal in all occupations, but the romanticism is more obvious in the sentence of the *Moral Sentiments* about the beggar who suns himself at the side of the road and has more security than kings who go to war.

Professor Donald Winch has drawn my attention to a later essay by Viner, in which he gave a sounder account of the *Moral Sentiments* and queried his earlier charge of inconsistency – but only on the general ground that Smith worked from systems or models and shifted from one 'partial model' to another. Viner's article of 1927 declared that in the *Moral Sentiments* Smith was 'a purely speculative philosopher', reasoning from allegedly self-evident axioms and 'failing to compare his conclusions with the facts'. One is tempted to say that nothing could be further from the truth – until one remembers Buckle and Skarżyński. Viner's original view is certainly the reverse of the truth. Smith took it for granted that Hutcheson and Hume had conclusively refuted the rationalist theories of moral philosophy which relied on reasoning from supposedly self-evident axioms. In all his work Smith followed the method of empiricism, of taking the facts of experience as the basic data and reaching general propositions by induction from them. To be sure, the *Wealth of Nations* contains a vast mass of empirical data, including much quantitative material, which the *Moral Sentiments* cannot even begin to emulate. Nevertheless it is a feature of the ethics book that it relies, more than most of its genre, on examples from genuine experience, observed or gathered from works of history.

All this does not mean that the enterprise of comparing the two books is mistaken. The earlier commentators were right in thinking that the concept of sympathy is the pivot of *The Theory of Moral Sentiments*. There is indeed a need to compare the role of sympathy in that work with the role of self-interest in the *Wealth of Nations*. The comparison is best made in terms of sociology. Sympathy and imagination in the *Moral Sentiments* are the cement of human society in forming socializing attitudes. They produce approbation and disapprobation. Since pretty well all human beings enjoy esteem and dislike contempt, the effect of approbation and disapprobation is to induce conformity to social norms both in behaviour and in attitude. Even when the conscience of an individual differs from the prevalent attitude of those around him, it still, according to Smith, is a reflecting mirror of the attitude of spectators, but of spectators imagined to be as well informed as the person whom they are judging. Ethical feelings and ethical judgements reflect social solidarity and help to strengthen it.

A different kind of social bond, mutual dependence, is produced by the division of labour. We think of the author of the *Wealth of Nations* as emphasizing the role of economic man, everyone pursuing his own interest as a separate individual. We tend to forget, however, that Smith does this in the context of the need for co-operation. When Smith says that we expect the butcher, brewer, and baker to provide our dinner from self-interest, not from benevolence, he is talking about the importance of exchange. We all need the help of other people. To get it, we do not rely on their benevolence; we think of ways in which we can help them in return and we expect them to respond to that. Although Smith emphasizes the motive of self-interest, his purpose is to show us the character, and also the extent, of mutual dependence in society. The same thing comes out in his metaphor of the invisible hand. The workings of the market bring it about that the self-interested actions of individuals contribute to the benefit of all, or at any rate to the benefit of most. It is the social consequences that matter, not the individualistic cause.

The social bond created by sympathy and imagination, which plays so important a part in the *Moral Sentiments*, is quite different from the social bonds of mutual dependence described in the *Wealth of Nations* as resulting both from the division of labour and from the workings of the market. It is different but it is not inconsistent with them. The social bond of sympathy and imagination leads to our code of ethics and to a good part of our code of law. Economic behaviour, on the other hand, has to be explained in terms of self-interest. This does not imply that a person engaged in economic transactions has no regard to what other people will think of him. Apart from anything else, economic exchange depends on contract, and the legal notions about the duties and rights of contract are as much tied up with ethics as they are with economics. But in economic life the thought of social approval and disapproval takes second place to the idea of doing the best for oneself. Nevertheless, the economic motive of doing the best for oneself does in fact result in a different form of social solidarity, mutual dependence.

The sociological dimension of Smith's thought can be seen also in other parts of the *Wealth of Nations*; it is still more prominent in the *Lectures on Jurisprudence*, and can be seen to some extent even in the *Lectures on Rhetoric*. Parts of Book V of the *Wealth of Nations* are far more sociological than economic. The section about the State's duty to administer justice incorporates a summary version of Smith's theory of the four stages of society, a theory which explains that law and government proper arise in the second stage, the age of shepherds. This theory has a much larger place in the *Lectures on Jurisprudence* because Smith's main subject there is the history of law and government, economics being treated as one part of the conduct of government. Smith's emphasis upon the role of property undoubtedly foreshadows the economic interpretation of the history of society that is so prominent in Marxist thought. Recent scholarship has questioned the attribution to Smith of a 'materialist' or economic interpretation of history because Smith is not a strict determinist and also because he regards vanity as fundamentally a more influential motive than the desire for material goods. The fact remains, however, that in his account of the origin of law and government Smith highlights the causal role of property to a remarkable degree.

I should also say that the age of shepherds is that where government first commences. Property makes it absolutely necessary. . . . In the age of the hunters a few temporary exertions of the authority of the community will be sufficient for the few occasions of dispute which can occur. Property, the grand fund of all dispute, is not then known. . . . But here [i.e. in the age of shepherds] when . . . some have great wealth and others nothing, it is necessary that the arm of authority should be continually stretched forth, and permanent laws or regulations made which may ascertain [i.e. secure] the property of the rich from the inroads of the poor . . . Laws and government may be considered . . . as a combination of the rich to oppress the poor, and preserve to themselves the inequality of the goods which would otherwise be soon destroyed by the attacks of the poor. (J 208, session 1762-3)

The appropriation of herds and flocks, which introduced an inequality of fortune, was that which first gave rise to regular government. Till there be property there can be no government, the very end of which is to secure wealth, and to defend the rich from the poor. (J 404, session 1763-4)

The acquisition of valuable and extensive property . . . necessarily requires the establishment of civil government. Where there is no property, or at least none that exceeds the value of two or three days labour, civil government is not so necessary. (W 710)

It is in the age of shepherds, in the second period of society, that the inequality of fortune first begins to take place, and introduces among men a degree of authority and subordination which could not possibly exist before. It thereby introduces some degree of that civil government which is indispensably necessary for its own preservation . . . Civil government, so far as it is instituted for the security of property, is in reality instituted for the defence of the rich against the poor, or of those who have some property against those who have none at all. (W 715)

Later in the *Wealth of Nations* Smith foreshadows an economic interpretation of particular historical events in explaining why the sophists of ancient Greece were *itinerant* teachers, and why fixed academies grew up later.

The demand for philosophy and rhetorick was for a long

time so small, that the first professed teachers of either could not find constant employment in any one city, but were obliged to travel about from place to place. In this manner lived Zeno of Elea, Protagoras, Gorgias, Hippias, and many others. As the demand increased, the schools both of philosophy and rhetorick became stationary; first in Athens, and afterwards in several other cities. (W 777)

Then again when he comes to discuss the role of the clergy, Smith sees an economic factor in the practices of the Roman Catholic priesthood.

In the church of Rome, the industry and zeal of the inferior clergy is kept more alive by the powerful motive of self-interest, than perhaps in any established protestant church. The parochial clergy derive, many of them, a very considerable part of their subsistence from the voluntary oblations of the people; a source of revenue which confession gives them many opportunities of improving. The mendicant orders derive their whole subsistence from such oblations. It is with them, as with the hussars and light infantry of some armies; no plunder, no pay. (W 789-90)

Smith shows a more broadly sociological outlook in his discussions of social class. In the *Moral Sentiments* he explains social status ('the distinction of ranks') as the result of sympathetic pleasure in the comforts of 'the rich and the great'. At the same time he notes that this form of approbation is apt to corrupt our properly moral approbation for wisdom and virtue. Admiration of the rich and the great leads them to care more for fashion and status ('the honour of exalted station') than for genuine virtue. In the *Wealth of Nations* Smith puts the last point in a slightly different way, relating two different codes of morality to two social classes. There is one moral code, 'the strict or austere', which is 'generally admired and revered by the common people', and there is another, 'the liberal, or, if you will, the loose system', which is 'commonly more esteemed and adopted by what are called people of fashion' (W 794).

The *Lectures on Jurisprudence* show a sociological bent throughout. Before they reach the final section on economics, they consist of a history, sociology, and philosophy of law and, to a lesser extent, of government. The three aspects go together. For Adam Smith, history and comparative sociology are the evidence from which to reach philosophical (or scientific) generalizations. However, the sociological aspect seems to come to the fore most frequently. For instance, when Smith discusses family law he shows a deep interest in the sociology of marriage and divorce, the status of women, and the historical changes in the social power of men as husbands, fathers, and heads of extended families. The most striking example, however, carried over into the *Wealth of Nations*, is his preoccupation with slavery – as a social, not just a legal, phenomenon. He is of course interested in the economics of slavery and believes that 'The experience of all ages and nations . . . demonstrates that the work done by slaves, though it appears to cost only their maintenance, is in the end the dearest of any' (W 387). But he is more profoundly moved by the persistently widespread practice of slavery.

> We are apt to imagine that slavery is entirely abolished at this time, without considering that this is the case in only a small part of Europe; not remembering that all over Moscovy and all the eastern parts of Europe, and the

whole of Asia, that is, from Bohemia to the Indian Ocean, all over Africa, and the greatest part of America, it is still in use. It is indeed allmost impossible that it should ever be totally or generally abolished. (J 181)

Smith's sociological interests can be seen even in his *Lectures on Rhetoric*. Professor W. S. Howell has shown that the most important feature of these lectures is their independence of tradition in widening the scope of the theory of rhetoric and adapting it to the needs of the time. This goes along with a sensitivity to the way in which different kinds of discourse are suited to the needs of different forms of society. 'The most barbarous and rude nations', such as those 'on the coast of Africa', Smith said, spend their leisure hours on dancing and singing together. For this they need to cultivate poetry but not prose. 'Tis the Introduction of Commerce or at least of opulence which is commonly the attendent of Commerce which first brings on the improvement of Prose' (R 137). Smith went on to suggest that differences in style between the speeches of Demosthenes and those of Cicero, or between the philosophical dialogues of Plato and those of Cicero, were related to the different social structures of Athens and Rome at the relevant times.

The Nobleman of Rome . . . would see . . . 1000 who were his inferiors for one who was even his equalls . . . As he spoke generally to his inferiors he would talk in a manner becoming one in that Station. . . . His discourse would be pompous and ornate and such as appeard to be the language of a superior sort of man.
  At Athens on the other hand the Citizens were all on equall footing; the greatest and the meanest were considered as being noway distinguished, and lived and

talkd together with the greatest familiarity. . . . It is observed that there is no Politeness or Compliments in the Dialogues of Plato; whereas those of Cicero abound with them. . . .

These considerations may serve to explain many of the differences in the manners and Stile of Demosthenes and Cicero. – The latter talks with the Dignity and authority of a superior and the former with the ease of an equall. (R 158-9)

In all his sociological discussions Smith draws his evidence from history and from such social anthropology as was available to him. That is to say, he used the comparative method. Like other thinkers of the Scottish Enlightenment, he learned the method from Montesquieu. He also took some of his evidence from Montesquieu, but he added a great deal more from other sources. The range of his evidence for comparative law, for example, is much wider than one would suppose. He had as a matter of course a fair stock of knowledge about Roman and Scots law. He acquired in addition a reasonable knowledge of English law and put it to good use for purposes of comparison. One also finds, however, in his *Lectures on Jurisprudence*, references to particular laws or institutions in ancient Athens and Sparta, ancient Germany (as reported by Tacitus), among the Hebrews of the Old Testament, the 'Tartars', the tribes of the Guinea coast, and the American Indians, in modern France, Holland, Switzerland, Lombardy, Russia ('Moscovy'), Venice, the East Indies, Persia, Turkey, Egypt, China, and Japan. As any modern sociologist would agree, the comparative method is a thoroughly sound way of trying to reach scientific generalizations. This needs to be borne in mind when one considers Smith's attitude to nature and natural law. His evidence was often insufficient to give scientific backing to his hypotheses; but the errors to which he was led by his use of the comparative method are less gross than those of the commentators, discussed earlier in this chapter, who misunderstood the evidence in their comparisons of the *Moral Sentiments* with the *Wealth of Nations*.

6   Philosophy, science, and history

'Scratch a Scotsman and you will find a philosopher', says the old adage. Tom Stoppard gave it continued currency when, in his play *Jumpers*, he made the Scottish university porter as acute at philosophical criticism as the Professor of Moral Philosophy. Perhaps Adam Smith had such a porter in mind when he said that the native abilities of a philosopher and a porter were almost equal (J 348, 493). The Scottish university tradition of philosophy for all had in fact a marked impact in the eighteenth century and infected the thought of a wide variety of educated men. The lectures of a leading scientist like Joseph Black no less than the books of a leading lawyer like Lord Kames contain an undercurrent of genuine philosophical enquiry. Adam Smith himself began his professional career as a philosopher and remained a philosopher all his life. While it turned out that his finest gifts lay in the field of economics and social science, he never lost his philosophical interests. As late as 1785 he was still planning to complete 'a sort of philosophical history' of literature and philosophy, and in his last years he gave a great deal of effort to the revision and expansion of the *Moral Sentiments*. According to Sir Samuel Romilly, he 'always considered his *Theory of Moral Sentiments* a much superior work to his *Wealth of Nations*'. If he did, his judgement was at fault but the report confirms his abiding love for philosophical enquiry.

Smith would not have recognized any clear distinction between philosophy and the social sciences, or for that matter between philosophy and natural science. Generally speaking, he uses the two terms 'philosophy' and 'science' almost interchangeably. There is one place in the *Wealth of Nations* (796) where he appears to imply a distinction between them, writing of 'the study of science and philosophy'. He goes on in the same paragraph to say that 'Science is the great antidote to the poison of enthusiasm and superstition'. He has been talking about religion and religious ethics; the phrase 'enthusiasm and superstition' means religion. Earlier in the chapter Smith has said that much post-Christian moral philosophy has pandered to absurd doctrines of religion. I think this is why he now implies a distinction between philosophy and science. Some philosophy can be irrational, and so Smith, for the moment, thinks of science as not quite the same; it is that kind of enquiry which conforms to empirical fact. Generally, however, Smith would call such enquiry a form of philosophy, reputable philosophy, whether it was dealing with the material world or with human behaviour.

For Smith, a 'philosopher' is a reflective observer, who can think of connections that allow theoretical explanation or practical invention. He gives a virtual definition in the first chapter of the *Wealth of Nations* (21), where he writes of inventions being made by 'those who are called philosophers or men of speculation, whose trade it is, not to do any thing, but to observe every thing; and who, upon that account, are often capable of combining together the powers of the most distant and dissimilar objects'. His 'philosophers or men of speculation' are not just armchair speculators, although they are contrasted with men of action. James Watt, no less than Sir Isaac Newton, is a 'philosopher', as Smith uses the term. In corresponding passages of earlier versions of this thought, Smith refers to the 'philosopher' who invented the 'fire engine' or 'fire machine' (J 347, 349, 492, 570). Scientists and technologists, no less than philosophers in the modern sense of the word, are 'men of speculation' who have the leisure to observe widely and to make connections which would not occur to others. The connections may be physical, metaphysical, or social. In the *Wealth of Nations* (674) Smith refers to Quesnay as 'a physician, and a very speculative physician', because he thought of 'the political body' after the analogy of the human body. In the *Moral Sentiments* (136) Smith imagines what our reaction would be if the whole of China were destroyed by an earthquake: after initial sorrow for the widespread distress, a 'man of speculation' might 'enter into many reasonings concerning the effects which this disaster might produce upon the commerce of Europe, and the trade and business of the world in general'. If it were Voltaire thinking about the Lisbon earthquake, he would reflect on the implications for theology. If it were Adam Smith, he would reflect on the implications for the world economy.

Philosophy, science, and social science were all the same sort of activity for Smith. In the manuscript that W. R. Scott has called an 'Early Draft' of the first part of the *Wealth of Nations*, Smith has a list of different kinds of 'philosophers' – 'mechanical, chymical, astronomical, physical, metaphysical, moral, political, commercial, and critical [i.e. writers on literary theory and aesthetics]' (J 570). They all have the same sort of aim, to make connections between diverse phenomena, but they do not all pursue the same sort of method in finding the relevant phenomena. All rely on observation, their own and that of others. Most natural scientists, however, will not need to depend much on the recorded observations of the past, i.e. on history, and can often repeat in their own laboratories observations reported by others. Social scientists have to rely much more on history and on the reported observations of others in addition to their own. Adam Smith was a keen, and generally an accurate, observer but he knew very well that his own observations could supply only a minute portion of the data he needed, whether for economics or sociology or moral philosophy. In all three areas he relied heavily on historical investigation as well as on the reports of contemporary enquirers. As I have said in Chapter 2, his favoured method of finding his feet in a subject was to study its history and then, after critical examination of earlier theories, to make his own contribution by improving upon them. The purpose of Smith's historical investigations, whether he was studying the history of events or the history of theories, was to acquire the data necessary to back up or refute a generalization, a hypothesis about a possible scientific law.

Soon after the death of Adam Smith, Dugald Stewart wrote an account of his life and writings for the Royal Society of Edinburgh. It was then reprinted as an introduction to Smith's *Essays on Philosophical Subjects*, published in 1795. In the course of it Stewart coined the phrase 'theoretical or conjectural history' to describe Smith's procedure in much of his work. Stewart was led to his remarks on this topic when he came to record the printing of an essay by Smith, 'Considerations concerning the First Formation of Languages', as an appendix to the third (Stewart said the second) and subsequent editions of the *Moral Sentiments*. The essay is worked up from a shorter treatment of the subject in Smith's lectures on rhetoric. Stewart said that while this essay on the origin and development of languages was interesting in its own right for its ingenuity, it deserved attention more, in his survey of Smith's work, 'as a specimen of a particular sort of inquiry' which could be 'traced in all his different works, whether moral, political, or literary' (P 292). Stewart did not, however, suggest that 'theoretical or conjectural history' was peculiar to Smith; he said it had been pursued by several modern thinkers from Montesquieu onwards. But the phrase has stuck in subsequent discussion of Adam Smith.

The adjective 'conjectural' is misleading if taken (as it has been by some) to imply that Smith invented some of his data and called the result history. One could say this of the essay on languages, which does include a good deal of speculation based simply on logical categories – though it also makes use of empirical facts about the languages which Smith knew and it is trying to make its way towards a scientific comparative philology concerning the structure of Greek and Latin and that of modern European languages. One might also say that the four stages theory of the history of society reaches its hypothesis of historical sequence on the basis of rather scanty evidence. There is, however, very little that is speculative or conjectural in Smith's other historical discussions, whether of ethical theory, of law and government, or of science and metaphysics. Stewart explicitly mentioned Smith's essay on the history of astronomy (together with a comparable, slightly later, history of mathematics by the French scholar J. E. Montucla) as an example of what he meant by 'theoretical history'; he used the alternative adjective 'conjectural' only once, when introducing the description, and then continued with 'theoretical history' alone. There is absolutely nothing conjectural about Smith's *history* of astronomy. It consists of firm, and on the whole reliable, data of definite empirical fact about the various theories of astronomy which have been held from Eudoxus to Newton. The essay, however, can properly be called a theoretical history (or better, as Smith described the unfulfilled project which would have included it, 'a sort of philosophical history') because it draws on the history of science as evidence for a philosophy of science. Similarly, one may say, Smith uses the history of law, government, and economics as evidence for generalizations in the theory or philosophy of law, government, and economics.

The essay on the history of astronomy shows us how Smith viewed the relation between history and theory. We should remember that he, like others of his time, made no clear distinction between philosophy and science. When he used historical evidence to support generalizations in 'political economy', present-day scholars might call those generalizations theories or hypotheses in 'economic science' or 'political science'. So far as Smith was concerned, there was no difference of substance between the principles for making headway in 'natural philosophy' and those for making headway in 'moral philosophy', including 'jurisprudence' and 'political economy'. As we shall see, the process requires the use of imagination, and so one may say that Stewart's suggestion of conjecture was not altogether misplaced; but Stewart did mislead by implying that the conjecture or imagination was used to supply missing historical data. Smith's view is that imagination is needed to fill up the gaps in a proposed *system*, a theory or model which tries to unify the data obtained by observation. Moreover, it is an exercise of imagination that is to be found in science at its best.

Smith's long essay 'The History of Astronomy', in *Essays on Philosophical Subjects*, deserves to rank with the *Wealth of Nations* and the *Moral Sentiments* as the work of an outstanding mind. In writing it Smith was one of the originators of the history and philosophy of science. On the historical side the work is remarkably well informed for its time and even today its information remains largely accurate. It is also genuinely philosophical, both in the pattern which it draws out of the historical facts and even more in its explanation of the changes from one type of scientific theory to another.

Smith starts off with the traditional view of Plato and Aristotle that philosophy (or science) begins in wonder. But he immediately elaborates this into a psychological theory that intellectual discomfort with what is unfamiliar leads on to the removal of the discomfort when we can find connections again with what is familiar. A modern scholar might describe the situation with the statement that an apparently unusual event is explained by showing it to be, not an isolated individual thing, but an instance of a general law. Smith concentrates on the psychological effects, first of surprise at the oddity, and then of relief at assimilating it with the familiar after all. A scientific theory (in astronomy or anything else) satisfies by removing intellectual discomfort at oddity. But oddity is not the only reason for intellectual discomfort. If we are to feel at ease with a recurring pattern, it must be relatively simple. Once it becomes complex, the recurrences are less easy to grasp, less familiar, and so less comfortable. When a scientific theory (for instance the Ptolemaic account of astronomy) has grown very complex in order to accommodate all the observed phenomena, we are dissatisfied once more and are prepared to welcome a different, simpler, sort of theory (like the Copernican). But of course the simplicity may have to be bought at a price. In the case of the Copernican theory we have a simpler pattern but we must adjust ourselves to a new suggestion which is exceedingly unfamiliar, namely that the Earth is in motion. So we need a development of theory which will remove our discomfort, indeed our shock, at that unfamiliarity.

This psychological explanation of the development of science or philosophy is itself, for Adam Smith, a piece of philosophy. It is in line with the interpretation of philosophy that he learned from Hume. At the heart of Smith's explanation is an account of the functions of the imagination, which comes straight out of Hume but is adapted from Hume's theory of our belief in a persisting external world and is used instead to show how scientific theory builds a framework to fit on to observed phenomena. Hume had said that the imagination fills in the gaps between observed 'impressions' (the data of perception) so as to produce the supposition of a permanent object. For example, I see a white oblong shape in front of me at 10.05; I go away, and when I come back at 10.10, I see a similar white oblong shape. My imagination fills in the gaps which occur in a series of such impressions and gives me the idea of a continuing material object, a sheet of paper, which exists both when I am in this place looking at it and when I am not. Smith adapted Hume's theory so as to apply it to scientific hypotheses about unobserved entities. The imagination fills in the gaps between observed phenomena (such as the Sun, the Moon, the Planets, and the Fixed Stars) and produces the supposition of a great 'machine' (such as a system of crystalline spheres containing the observed heavenly bodies but being themselves unobservable because they are crystalline and so transparent).

Smith evidently regards all scientific and philosophical systems as products of the imagination.

Systems in many respects resemble machines. A machine is a little system, created to perform, as well as to connect together, in reality, those different movements and effects which the artist [i.e. the practical man, as contrasted with the theorist] has occasion for. A system is an imaginary machine invented to connect together in the fancy those different

> movements and effects which are already in reality performed. (P 66)

Scientific theories or systems are imagined structures which connect together observed movements and other events. The systems are not themselves actualities of nature, or at least we cannot know them to be such. A theory or system is preferred, Smith says, because it suits the propensities of the human mind, not because it is the only one which accommodates the observed phenomena.

He was struck especially by the change of attitude among scientists towards Descartes's theory of vortices. As Smith saw the history of astronomy, the Copernican hypothesis scored over its predecessors by its simplicity but faced an enormous psychological obstacle with its implication that the Earth was subject to two sets of motion at very high speed. The difficulty was not the mere idea that the Earth was in motion, contrary to all appearances of rest. For the learned at least, the trouble was rather that earlier theory had represented any motion of ponderous bodies as slow, while the Copernican hypothesis required us to suppose that the daily rotation of the Earth round its own axis meant, for any point on the equator, a speed of a thousand miles an hour, faster than a cannon-ball or even than the speed of sound, and that the orbital motion of the Earth round the Sun was faster still. Descartes's theory of vortices became popular because it tried 'to render familiar to the imagination, the greatest difficulty in the Copernican system, the rapid motion of the enormous bodies of the Planets' (P 96). In due course, however, Newton's system gave a more satisfying account and Descartes's theory became an 'exploded hypothesis'.

Consequently Smith was quite ready to understand that Newton's theory might not be the last word. He ended his essay by recalling, with some difficulty, that his account of science as the work of the imagination must apply to Newton's theory no less than to earlier systems.

> And even we, while we have been endeavouring to represent all philosophical systems as mere inventions of the imagination . . . have insensibly been drawn in, to make use of language expressing the connecting principles of this one, as if they were the real chains which Nature makes use of to bind together her several operations. Can we wonder then, that it should have gained the general and complete approbation of mankind, and that it should now be considered, not as an attempt to connect in the imagination the phaenomena of the Heavens, but as the greatest discovery that ever was made by man, the discovery of an immense chain of the most important and sublime truths, all closely connected together, by one capital fact, of the reality of which we have daily experience. (P 105)

It was indeed a remarkable feat on the part of Adam Smith to be able, in the 1750s, to think of Newton's account of the solar system as a theory that could be replaced, and not as a statement of objective fact. He could do so because of his view that all theoretical systems depend on the imagination.

There is no reason to suppose that Smith regarded systems of economic theory as any different in this respect from systems of natural philosophy. One may be tempted to think otherwise when one recalls his remark that the physiocratic system was 'the nearest approximation to the truth' that had previously been published in economics. This seems to imply that there is a 'truth' to be reached. But it is simply a natural way to speak when you are immersed in a discussion of the relative merits of different theories in a particular discipline. Smith certainly thought that the physiocratic system was superior to mercantilism in its explanation of the observed facts, just as he thought, like everyone else, that the Newtonian system was superior to that of Descartes. He noted in 'The History of Astronomy' that he had been naturally led, like others, to speak of the Newtonian system as a discovery of objective truth. So too in the *Moral Sentiments* he wrote that a system of natural philosophy, such as that of Descartes, may be accepted for a long time 'and yet have no foundation in nature, nor any sort of resemblance to the truth' (M 313). This implies that the system of Newton does have a foundation in nature and at least a resemblance to the truth. But when Smith stands back and considers the whole class of theoretical systems, he distinguishes them from the actual, or at any rate the knowable, facts of nature.

It follows, then, that Smith would say of his own system of economics what he says of the Newtonian system of astronomy. It is sounder than its predecessors but it is still a theoretical system, a product of the imagination, not a description of 'real chains which Nature makes use of to bind together her several operations'. The 'gravitating' of market prices towards the natural price, the 'invisible hand' which 'leads' self-interested agents to promote the public interest, the apparent force of 'natural liberty' and 'natural equality' – these are all products of the imagination which help us to connect observable facts but are not themselves facts or realities that might be observable or otherwise knowable. Nevertheless they are, in Smith's view, an aid to understanding; in order to make connections, science needs its 'imaginary machines'. The author of the *Wealth of Nations* is of a piece with the philosopher who wrote 'The History of Astronomy' and *The Theory of Moral Sentiments*. The *Wealth of Nations* is his masterpiece and shines by its own light, but it is further illuminated when it is linked with the other two works.

References

3   *Letters of James Boswell*, ed. C. B. Tinker (Oxford, 1924), 46; quoted by J. C. Bryce, introduction to *Lectures on Rhetoric and Belles Lettres*, *34*.

7   Edward Westermarck, *Ethical Relativity* (London, 1932), 71.

7   H. T. Buckle, *History of Civilization in England* (London, 1857-61), i. 194; cf. ii. 443.

8   John Rae, *Life of Adam Smith* (London, 1895), 5.

15   Ibid. 57.

16   Ibid. 170, quoting A. F. Tytler.

20   Ibid. 211-12.

23   Ibid. 287.

27   Ibid. 405.

35   A. L. Macfie, *The Individual in Society* (London, 1967), 66.

72   The log of the *Prince George*, quoted by Ronald Faux, 'Swallowed in the Swirling Sarcophagus', *The Times*, 16 Oct. 1982, Saturday Supplement, 1.

83   J. A. Schumpeter, *History of Economic Analysis* (New York, 1954), 184-5, 187, 182.

88   H. T. Buckle, op. cit. ii. 432-3, 437.

89   W. von Skarzyński, *Adam Smith als Moralphilosoph und Schoepfer der Nationaloekonomie* (Berlin, 1878), 6-7, 53.

90   Jacob Viner, 'Adam Smith and Laissez Faire', *Journal of Political Economy* xxxv (1927); reprinted in Viner, *The Long View and the Short* (Glencoe, Ill., 1958).

92   Jacob Viner, 'Adam Smith', in *International Encyclopedia of the Social Sciences* (New York, 1968).

95 Determinism and 'materialism': see Donald Winch, *Adam Smith's Politics* (Cambridge, 1978), 57, 81; and more particularly Knud Haakonssen, *The Science of a Legislator* (Cambridge, 1981), 181-7.

99 W. S. Howell, 'Adam Smith's Lectures on Rhetoric: An historical assessment', *Speech Monographs* xxxvi (Nov. 1969); reprinted in *Essays on Adam Smith*, ed. Andrew S. Skinner and Thomas Wilson (Oxford, 1975).

102 Sir Samuel Romilly, *Memoirs* (London, 1840), i. 403; quoted by Rae, op. cit. 436.

104 W. R. Scott, *Adam Smith as Student and Professor* (Glasgow, 1937), xxii, 317.

Further reading

The *Wealth of Nations*, *The Theory of Moral Sentiments*, and 'The History of Astronomy' (in *Essays on Philosophical Subjects*) are all works which can be read with pleasure by non-specialists. They are edited with textual and explanatory notes and introductions in The Glasgow Edition of the Works and Correspondence of Adam Smith (Oxford, 1976-83). The *Wealth of Nations* was admirably edited for an earlier generation by Edwin Cannan in 1904 (London) and his introduction and notes are still of great value. Undergraduate students of economics will probably find it most convenient, as well as economical, to acquire the Pelican Classics volume containing Books I-III of the *Wealth of Nations*, edited by Andrew Skinner (Harmondsworth, 1970) with a long, lucid introduction.

John Rae's *Life of Adam Smith* (London, 1895; reprinted with additional material by Jacob Viner, New York, 1965) is very enjoyable and quite comprehensive for its time. A new biography is being written by Ian S. Ross and will be associated with the Glasgow edition of Smith's works. The biographical chapters of *Adam Smith* by R. H. Campbell and A. S. Skinner (London, 1982) contain a good deal of new information that was not available to Rae (or Viner). This book also includes clear, concise surveys of Adam Smith's writings and lectures. It can be thoroughly recommended to all readers – not only novices – who are interested in Adam Smith. A similar short book, *Adam Smith: The man and his works* by E. G. West (New York, 1969), is lively but not always accurate.

For Smith's ethics the one indispensable work of

interpretation is T. D. Campbell, *Adam Smith's Science of Morals* (London, 1971).

The amount of published commentary on the *Wealth of Nations* is enormous. For relative beginners I would recommend particularly: Andrew S. Skinner, *A System of Social Science: Papers relating to Adam Smith* (Oxford, 1979), and Mark Blaug, *Economic Theory in Retrospect* (Homewood, Ill., 1962, but preferably the third edition, Cambridge, 1978), ch. 2. Blaug's chapter is not only for beginners; it also relates Smith's theories to those of later economists in a fairly sophisticated way. Samuel Hollander, *The Economics of Adam Smith* (Toronto, 1973), is a more elaborate discussion, though not easy reading. *The Market and the State: Papers in honour of Adam Smith*, edited by Thomas Wilson and Andrew S. Skinner (Oxford, 1976), reviews themes of the *Wealth of Nations* as they appear in our own time.

Another collection, associated with the Glasgow edition of Smith's works, *Essays on Adam Smith*, edited by Andrew S. Skinner and Thomas Wilson (Oxford, 1975), deals with all aspects of Adam Smith's writing and teaching.

Index